Abundance

ABUNDANCE

Creating a Culture of Generosity

MICHAEL R. WARD

Fortress Press

Minneapolis

ABUNDANCE
Creating a Culture of Generosity

Print ISBN: 978-1-5064-6140-3
eBook ISBN: 978-1-5064-6142-7

Cover image: Hands herb one line/iStock.com/undefined undefined; White recycled paper sheet/iStock.com/jessicahyde
Cover design: Lauren Williamson

To Caroline and Luke, with a prayer that the church will always be a place where you recognize God's abundant love for you in your life

And to Hannah, for your abundant support, which has allowed me to engage this work and discover these stories of God's abundance

CONTENTS

INTRODUCTION

We believe in a God of abundance, but along with our congregations we often reflect a scarcity mindset. Sometimes this is intentional as we are tricked to believe that people are stimulated to give by telling them we are out of money. The scarcity mindset is unfaithful to our God who is creator and still creating in our world today. Often, we don't recognize that what we say and do models a God who is finished with creation and that we live in a world where we don't have enough. This is not the God of our creeds nor of our biblical understanding, nor is it the God I encounter in our world day to day. Often, congregations reinforce a scarcity mentality when they

- publish a box score in the bulletin where expenses exceed revenue;
- celebrate keeping a budget flat;
- assume they have to cut expenses instead of raising gift income;
- hire only part-time staff to save on benefits;
- live in the past and not envision a brighter future;
- seek to survive rather than thrive;

- utilize volunteers without any accountability for key positions;

- accept mediocrity; or

- build up "reserves" out of fear for the future rather than investing in the mission of the ministry.

Many nonchurch institutions model a better path that congregations can learn from. These institutions

- know their mission;

- create visions that are worthy of investment;

- focus significantly on board and staff development;

- invite people to partner with them through financial generosity through bold asks that grow generosity;

- are willing to invest in the future and take risk; and

- believe that there are enough resources in the world to accomplish their vision as long as they work to discover where they are.

Jesus came and lived among us. He died on the cross for us, and the tomb is empty. If God can empty a tomb, certainly God can provide us with what we need for our mission and ministry.

My mother will tell you that I have been good at asking for money from a very young age. However, I also learned from her that it is by asking for gifts that ministry expands. We were members of a mission congregation when I was growing up. I recall that the congregation had a campaign to buy pews when I was in my mid-teens. Dad is Catholic and didn't worship with us, so Mom asked me to join her in giving a pew to the church. She asked me to give half of the pew, and because she asked, I did. We did our part, and it was joyful to make that gift together.

We don't have to live in a church that assumes there isn't enough to make an impact. Jesus fed five thousand with five loaves of bread and two fish, with much left over. Let's be a church that believes there will be leftovers and that we can even put those leftovers to good use. Let's be a church that demands excellence and strives to be relevant and impactful in the world. Let's be leaders in a church that understands its place in our culture today and how to position itself to reach that culture with the good news of Jesus.

Not only do I want to live in this world, I believe that it is coming into being. In 2018, my firm and over 150 congregations walked across the country for annual stewardship drives through a program we call Stewardship for All Seasons (SAS). These congregations are reporting the potential of an additional $4 million to be given by their members for their missions in 2019. This is an average increase of over $25,000 per congregation. At least five congregations grew by more than $100,000 for the year. A smaller congregation grew 20 percent from $150,000 to $180,000. Many grew for the first time in decades. One congregation I have worked with for the last four years has nearly doubled their annual income in that time, and the culture has changed significantly. The tomb is empty. Congregations can and do grow dramatically in their stewardship for annual ministry.

When I hear people talk about scarcity, all I can say is that is not my experience. We need to be careful that we don't create our own destiny with this scarcity talk.

If we say there isn't enough, there won't be. I also recognize that it is harder in some communities than others, but I think abundance can happen anywhere. For example, a congregation in inner-city Milwaukee grew revenue 33 percent in the first year of our engagement. Let me define two important concepts.

Abundance: I believe that abundance is a mindset and not a condition of wealth. Abundance is recognizing the One who provides us everything and recognizing that it is not only enough, but enough to share.

Generosity: This is not only for the uberwealthy among us. In fact, much of the time those who are most generous are not the wealthiest. The generous are the ones who have learned that the joy of material wealth is the ability to share it with others for the common good with no expectation of receiving anything in return.

I have written this book to help you lead your congregation to live in the world of God's abundance. I pray that something here will help you envision a future of growth and lead people to recognize that we have a critical mission to the world as God's church. We have good news to share, and we have the resources to adapt so that we can engage the world with extreme effectiveness today. I do believe the best days for the church in the United States are ahead of us.

The primary challenge before us, in my opinion, is the pervading culture of scarcity in many congregations. Changing culture takes intentional work over time. I am not presenting a one-size-fits-all solution that suddenly produces a new culture. It takes systematic work day in and day out, but it can happen, and it can happen in all ministry contexts. The firm I work for has developed Ten

Steps to Success as a guide to leading any nonprofit organization to thrive. This book will primarily focus on the first three steps, as they are the building blocks to growth and vitality.

These Ten Steps are timeless in their theory, although they need to be reinterpreted and reimagined regularly in specific contexts to fit our world today. These steps also keep us from chasing trendy tactics and expecting that they will change culture. These steps, interpreted in your context, will lead you to a strong, vital, relevant organization serving your community and implementing your mission.

By the way, my hobby is beekeeping. I normally manage about fifteen hives in the mountains of North Carolina. Bees can teach us much about abundance and how to live believing in it. I will relate life in the hive to life in the church throughout the book.

CHAPTER 1.

GROUNDED

A bee colony is often referred to as a superorganism. No honeybee can live in isolation. A queen will die without attendants to feed and care for her. The workers will die off if the queen doesn't lay new eggs. The drones (male bees) are needed for fertilizing queens so that the colony can maintain a healthy leader. Worker bees leave the hive during the day, but they all return to the colony as the sun goes down. They are grounded in the belief that each will do their job and that together, they can be healthy and accomplish their number one goal which is to expand and thrive.

I served on the national board of my denomination. A report was presented at one of the meetings about the struggles of our seminaries. In that report, a statement was made that we need to remove the "burden" of fundraising from our seminaries. I couldn't believe that fundraising was referred to as a burden. I see it differently. Fundraising is life-giving. It brings purpose to people's lives. When we do it well, people see God differently, and our churches and organizations get advocates working on their behalf. Henri Nouwen, in *A Spirituality of Fundraising*, states, "Fundraising is proclaiming what we believe in such a way that we offer other people an opportunity to participate with us in our vision and mission."[1] Personally, I believe that our seminaries were struggling because they hadn't done fundraising well enough. I don't think they just needed the money. They needed a group of people, donors, who had their hearts closely aligned with their mission to make the organizations stronger and better represent the full kingdom of God here on earth.

We need to be able to articulate why we raise money. It is not simply to pay bills or give staff a bigger salary, although we may use gifts for that. We don't raise money to save an organization. God doesn't need all of our organizations, although I believe God can use most of them when our mission aligns with what God needs to have happen in our world today.

Biblically, I think we should ground our stewardship and fundraising efforts in Jesus's words from Matthew 6:21. Jesus says, "Where your treasure is, there your heart will be also." I was nearly done with seminary when I finally understood what Jesus meant. I thought that where our hearts were, our treasures naturally followed behind. I thought that if we got people to like the church more, they would give more. Jesus says that is backwards. It is where our treasures are that we will find our hearts. Think about your own life and where your treasure might be. Is it in travel soccer for your children, a vacation home, your car, or something else tangible in this world? As you ponder this, then think about whether Jesus is correct that your heart is tied into that item or activity. What has captured your heart, and where would you like your heart to be?

1. Henri Nouwen, *A Spirituality of Fundraising* (Nashville: Upper Room, 2011), 16.

The First Article of the Apostles' Creed and Martin Luther's Explanation is a great place to ground our theology of abundance.

I believe in God the Father almighty, creator of heaven and earth.
What is this? *or* What does this mean?
Answer: I believe that God has created me together with all that exists. God has given me and still preserves my body and soul: eyes, ears, and all limbs and senses; reason and all mental faculties.

In addition, God daily and abundantly provides shoes and clothing, house and farm, spouse and children, fields, livestock, and all property—along with the necessities and nourishment for this body and life. God protects me from and shields and preserves me from all evil. All this is done out of pure, fatherly, and divine goodness and mercy, without any merit or worthiness of mine at all! For all this I owe it to God to thank and praise, serve and obey him. This is most certainly true.[2]

Most Christians believe that God is the creator, as the first book of the Bible claims. It's one of the first faith stories we learn as children. However, in the United States, most Protestants have a difficult time articulating what Luther is saying here. If God *is* creator, that means we owe everything we have to God. Some of us don't care for this understanding because we like to get credit for our stuff and claim it as "ours." Our national or cultural "theology" in the United States is grounded in private property and ownership. However, if Luther is right, God is responsible for everything that we possess. It is all a gift from the giver.

In the book *Passing the Plate: Why American Christians Don't Give Away More Money*, the authors say, "Nearly

2. The Explanation to the First Article in *Luther's Small Catechism with Evangelical Lutheran Worship Texts* (Minneapolis: Augsburg Fortress, 2008), 36.

every Christian denomination and tradition has official teachings about financial giving, wealth, and stewardship intended to guide members in faithful practices concerning uses of income and wealth."[3] Here are some examples of those traditions that are mentioned in the book.

- In 2000 the Episcopal Church passed a resolution emphasizing tithing as the "minimum standard of giving" but also stated, "We believe: We are the children of God, and we need to give." So, in addition to the concept of tithing the denomination recognizes that the benefit to the giver is that they have a need to be generous to fully live.[4]

- The Presbyterian Church in America states, "The stewardship of our finances begins with the tithe."[5]

- The Presbyterian Church U.S.A. does speak of tithing and the practices of sacrifice but goes on to speak to the "proper management of the possessions that God has entrusted" us. The statement on stewardship theology from 2001 states, "We understand that all resources are God's and that they are to be used for God's purposes."[6]

- The Evangelical Lutheran Church in America (ELCA), in its document "Living Faith, ELCA-wide Call to Discipleship," states, "The maturing disciple is also maturing in financial stewardship, under-

3. Christian Smith, Michael O. Emerson, and Patricia Snell, *Passing the Plate: Why American Christians Don't Give Away More Money* (Oxford: Oxford University Press, 2008), 197.

4. Smith, Emerson, and Snell, *Passing the Plate*, 215.

5. Smith, Emerson, and Snell, *Passing the Plate*, 224.

6. Smith, Emerson, and Snell, *Passing the Plate*, 224–25.

stands the biblical tithe, and is growing in sacrificial and joyful giving toward and beyond a ten percent response in all areas of life. Part of the disciple's job description is to give freely."[7]

- The United Methodist Church, in the 2004 Book of Resolutions of the United Methodist Church, called for "preaching and teaching spiritual growth in giving, with an emphasis of setting tithing as a goal for every person in The United Methodist Church."[8]

Notice that I have not grounded stewardship in the idea of tithing, and yet most denominations speak of it in their key teachings on stewardship. Though tithing as a target is helpful for some Christians and certainly something to be lifted up on the discipleship journey, the reality is that fewer than 9.4 percent of Christians tithe.[9] I have not found that tithing motivates most people. A focus on the hearts of our people and growing those hearts closer to our ministry is more effective. I prefer to focus on a generosity journey rather than to think that we suddenly arrive at the endpoint that includes giving a tithe. The Bible talks about tithes *and* offerings. For the tither, offerings can be the continuation of the generosity journey. The key is for people to start the journey and not sit on the sidelines assuming they don't have anything to offer. An additional reality is that 22.1 percent of Christians give nothing to the church.[10] I would rather we not

7. Smith, Emerson, and Snell, *Passing the Plate*, 216.

8. Smith, Emerson, and Snell, *Passing the Plate*, 228.

9. Smith, Emerson, and Snell, *Passing the Plate*, 30.

10. Smith, Emerson, and Snell, *Passing the Plate*, 30.

ground stewardship in tithing because it is not helpful for the average church member, and it is an unrealistic and unattainable goal to reach for many. Reaching a goal of every member growing in generosity is a much more realistic and helpful goal.

Along with grounding stewardship and fundraising biblically and theologically, it is helpful to ground our work in some concepts beautifully articulated by Henri Nouwen. Nouwen's *A Spirituality of Fundraising* is one of my favorite resources to share with people to help them see that fundraising and stewardship has a deep spiritual principle and isn't just a "necessary evil" or even a "burden" of ministry. In the introduction to the book Nouwen shares that he initially thought of fundraising "as a necessary but unpleasant activity to support spiritual things." However, he later came to believe that "fundraising is first and foremost a form of ministry."[11]

Nouwen is right. Fundraising is ministry. The problem is too many of our stewardship models in the church have been ineffective, inefficient, and spiritually lacking. We have not built our tactics to be formational to faith. Stewardship appeals, special gift appeals, and capital campaigns should be spiritually renewing and not just a means to an end. They are ministry themselves. They are less about money and far more about people's hearts.

I have had the great pleasure to develop deeper relationships with people as a professional fundraiser than I did in my time as a parish pastor. The reason? When we discuss people's treasures, we are able to talk about what is closest to their hearts. This reality touched my own family as my mother made a gift to memorialize my two

___

11. Nouwen, *Spirituality of Fundraising*, vii.

brothers who died before I was born. As she made this gift, my mother shared with me most deeply the impact that these two sons had made on her life and the joy that she found by leaving a lasting memory to their lives. She experienced spiritual healing through her gift.

We engage in fundraising and stewardship because we want to connect people's hearts more deeply in the church and in our ministries. We engage in fundraising and stewardship because people need to have a healthy relationship with their money and recognize the One who allows them to use that money. And we engage in fundraising and stewardship because through this work, we engage in significant ministry with the people in our parishes who care for our ministry.

In the book *Passing the Plate*, the authors completed a sociological study of giving in the United States. Though the numbers are getting a bit dated, they are likely still very similar. The statistic cited above is worth repeating. They determined that approximately 9.4 percent of Christians are tithers or better, meaning they give 10 percent or more of their income to the church. Tithing has been a predominate theme in stewardship appeals in our churches over the years. With 90.6 percent of people not giving a tithe, it may be aspirational to think in terms of tithing, but it isn't motivational and is not helpful. To get an even clearer picture of the giving landscape in our churches, I often share the giving statistics of the median Protestant. The median is the person in the middle of the line if you put all of us in order from smallest giving percentage to largest. The study cited above also shows that the median protestant by giving percentage gives "only 0.62% of the median income of U.S.

Christians" to the church.[12] What this indicates is more than half of all of our church members give less than 1 percent of their income to charity. Therefore, instead of focusing on tithing, we should encourage each member of our congregation to grow in generosity. A small group in your congregation likely should learn about tithing and be challenged to reach a tithe and then move on to the concept of offerings after they reach the tithe. But for the majority of us, generosity should be a journey where we are consistently challenged to grow and expand what that means in our life.

JUST A DOZEN WORDS

My business partner Dave Brunkow wrote the following reflection on living as "First Article People."

> "I believe in God the Father almighty, Maker of heaven and earth."
>
> I remember a pastor who, when I was a youngster at Bible camp, talked to us about being "First Article People." I had no idea what he meant. In fact I might not even have had an inkling that he was talking about the first twelve words in the Apostles' Creed. I was not always attentive in confirmation class!
>
> But, as Pastor Myers explained, those first twelve words of the Creed are pretty powerful. He made the point that those words are the basis for all we believe as Christians.
>
> So, if we are indeed First Article People, what does this mean? (I do remember that question from confirmation!) I have mulled that over from time to time all my life, I think.
>
> When I speak these first twelve words, I have made a stupendous statement. "I believe that God has provided all that I see, that I am, that I eat and drink, that I have—all by which I am sustained."

12. Smith, Emerson, and Snell, *Passing the Plate*, 36.

In saying and believing this, I also am stating that everything comes from the Creator's hand without any merit, worthiness, or effort of my own. At this point one should stop and ponder the implications because they are at once disturbing and life shaping, depending on one's point of view.

If I cannot accept these twelve words as the truth, then I really can't move on to the Second and Third Articles. How could I really believe the divinity of Christ, and the accounts of his miracles and of his death and ultimate resurrection if I do not fully accept the fact that God is in control and providing all we need?

If I cannot accept the First Article as truth, how am I to believe that God can be fully present in spirit day in and day out, guiding and sustaining me in my work, in family life, and in all my actions and relationships?

How could I participate in the sacraments with a clear conscience? How could I speak words of consolation about God's presence to family and friends who are suffering, grieving, or struggling with in their lives?

Yes, in expressing the first twelve words of the Creed, we are going all in on truly being God's people. Now, of course, this does not mean that our faith is at all times unfaltering or that we live as convicted Christians every day of our lives. But it maybe means that we are focused on this belief as the central tenet of our life—that God is all.

Perhaps the strongest demonstrations of our belief are those acts of giving and sharing that we do. The ultimate act of belief may be the financial gifts we share in support of God's work since we would like to cling to the idea that our money is a direct result of our own merit, talent, hard work and good decision-making. Aren't we great! Of course, we feel this way!

So when we take our money to the altar, place it in an offering plate, or mail it in, we are witnessing to our belief as stated in the Creed. We are offering confirmation of our passion for the advancement of the gospel, and we are acknowledging that are first gift recipients of all we have and "own."

In many ways, getting past the First Article is a major stepping stone in acknowledgment that the Holy Spirit has moved us to acceptance of Christ and his resurrection. Our Christian faith is a tumultuous journey—at least it is for me. Coming to grips with the First Article through sincere and joyful giving is the lynchpin that keeps us grounded in that journey.

PART I.

THE TEN STEPS:
AN OVERVIEW

GSB Fundraising has utilized Ten Steps in working with clients since our firm was founded back in 1976. These steps are timeless, but how they are addressed evolves in every context. For the sake of this book, we will focus on steps 1–3, since they are the foundational steps for organizations seeking to live into abundance. Steps 4–10 will lead to achieving abundance and will perhaps be the basis of a future book. GSB partners and consultants often reflect on these steps in blogs, so if you are looking for more on those topics, follow www.gsbfr.com.

Ten Steps to Success
for Congregations

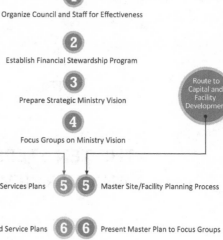

1 Organize Council and Staff for Effectiveness

2 Establish Financial Stewardship Program

Route to Ministry Development

3 Prepare Strategic Ministry Vision

Route to Capital and Facility Development

4 Focus Groups on Ministry Vision

Design Program and Services Plans	**5** **5**	Master Site/Facility Planning Process
Implement Program and Service Plans	**6** **6**	Present Master Plan to Focus Groups
Expand Annual Giving Program	**7** **7**	Feasibility Study
Enhance Marketing and Communications	**8** **8**	Capital Campaign
Build Calling Systems for Leadership Gifts	**9** **9**	Implement Building Projects
Begin and Expand Planned Giving for Endowment	**10** **10**	Expand Annual Giving and Endowment Programs

CHAPTER 2.

BOARD AND STAFF LEADERSHIP

In the bee colony, the queen is in charge. She produces pheromones to direct the colony in what to do. Without a good queen, the colony will collapse and die. However, she can't do it alone. An interesting fact is that if she doesn't lead well, the colony will replace her. As she leads, she knows if a nectar flow is coming and, if so, lays more eggs so the colony is as strong as possible. If bad times are ahead and there will be a dearth, she slows down her egg laying so that the colony does not have to feed as many bees when resources are lower. She adapts to the times.

Furthermore, each bee has a job to do. The first job of a newly hatched bee is to turn right around and clean out the cell from which they emerged so that the queen can lay another egg in the cell. Bees progress through a series of jobs until they are about three weeks old, and then they begin flying. After that, they gather pollen or nectar until they die.

Our churches and institutions need strong leadership from both board and staff. In congregations, we don't elect board members for their wealth, but we do elect them for leadership. Sadly, in many congregations, serving on the leadership board is often seen as a duty rather than an honor and delight. I think serving on a church's governing board can be the high point of someone's service in the church, but only if that board is effectively led. Many church judicatories elect their boards or councils based on gender, geographical district, and whether someone is ordained or not. This method of electing board or council members may be an efficient method, but ideally boards will be made up of people who also have the skills and the passion needed to do the work required. We can't train passion! Fortunately, many boards do understand this dynamic and have Board Development Committees that discern needed gifts, and they actively pursue those people they want in order to have a balanced, effective board.

Our individual congregations should look to our nonprofit counterparts for how to develop our boards. I have had nonprofit leaders tell me that they spend at least 10 percent of their time (four to five hours per week!) identifying, recruiting, and training board members.

When I work with congregations, we always spend at least a little time on how to have an effective governing board. If the board cannot be trusted and doesn't exude confidence, giving will not be as strong as it can be. If the mission and vision is not tended to by a strong board, an organization will wander aimlessly and not be worthy of the best gifts. "Boards of Trustees are supposed to be the ultimate guardians of institutional ethos and organizational values."[1]

1. Richard P. Chait, Willian P. Ryan, and Barbara E. Taylor, *Governance as Leadership: Reframing the Work of Non-Profit Boards* (Hoboken, NJ: Wiley 2004), 3.

LEADERSHIP BOARD AND STAFF FOCUS

Several pastors who served on the board for the camps where I was vice president of advancement credited their camp board experience in demonstrating to them how an effective board is able to function—with purpose and direction. They most frequently credited the clarity of their role, the specificity of the strategic plan to guide their work, and the attention to detail and training provided by the executive director as key lessons to take back to their congregations.

The board's role is to focus on the congregation's mission, vision, and strategic priorities. At the same time, staff and management should focus on goals, objectives, and tactics. In the congregation, depending on its size, sometimes "management" is staff, and sometimes management is a team of members of the congregation who take ownership of the goal. Most congregations do not have enough financial resources to turn implementation of each goal over to staff. By necessity, some board or committee members end up working on implementing strategies. In effect, they become part of the management team as volunteer staff. This has the potential to cause confusion.

If you read and reflect on your council minutes, you should be able to determine if you are focusing on the right activities. If the minutes talk about placing poinsettias around the church for Advent, you are in the middle of management activity. If the focus is on needing youth leaders for an upcoming retreat, the council is in management's role. However, if the focus is on the relationship between the congregation and the preschool, the council is focused on mission. Or if the work is attending to discerning how a new ministry aligns with current vision and strategic priorities, the council is mission-minded.

Council members need to take their calling to serve seriously. They have a duty to

- read material ahead of time;
- work ahead of meetings to resolve issues rather than to derail progress during a meeting;
- leave personal agendas behind;
- make the organization their number one philanthropic priority during their term of service;
- listen to the viewpoints of others;
- make decisions in the best interest of the organization;
- guard the mission of the organization and not allow for mission creep, that is, engaging in activities that do not align with your mission;
- become articulate in being able to describe the purpose and impact of the church; and
- work to assure that the mission is funded appropriately.

Some best practices for board meetings include the following.

- Every meeting should have a purpose. If a purpose for the meeting cannot be clearly identified, work should be invested in stating the purpose more clearly or creating a better strategic plan. The vision is likely too small if you cannot figure out a purpose to meet.

- Every item on the agenda should have a time allocation. Remember, what folks devote the most time to is that which is most important to them, whether that is intentionally stated or not. A vote to extend time if something needs more time is appropriate, but too often we spend too much time on the issues that are of least importance.

- Offer a consent agenda for reports. Leaders have a duty to read reports ahead of meetings. Don't waste people's time by reading things they can read themselves.

- Focus on the strategic plan and its implementation. Monitor how implementation is coming, and help remove roadblocks.

- Discuss and model leadership development.

- Grow spiritually as a result of the meeting.

- Share at least one ministry outcome since the last meeting, and practice sharing it. One of my favorite methods is for council members to call or write a note to one or two members sharing the outcome story and letting them know that their financial support is appreciated as you accomplish these outcomes. (For the difference in outcomes and activities, see chap. 6.)

- Evaluate every meeting and be willing to be honest with one another. For example, ask questions such as:
    ◦ Was the purpose of the meeting fulfilled?
    ◦ Were members fully present?

- Were people appropriately prepared both to present and to receive information?

- Did members learn of (or share) the ways in which God is active in the church and world?

- Were outcome stories shared of the ministry with a plan to share those stories with all the members?

- Did we focus on strategic level initiatives, or did we engage in the minutiae?

Staff alignment can be an issue in congregations as well. Staff supervision was the hardest part of my job when I was vice president of advancement at the Lutheran camps of the Southeast United States. However, one clear tactic led to more successful staff alignment: When we clearly articulated the goals of the position and how it fit our mission and our desired outcomes of the position, we did far better than when we simply said we need to hire a development officer.

The same is true in the church. Often, we say we need an associate pastor or a youth director or a communications specialist. We start the conversation with the position rather than the outcome desired. I have found that candidates for positions and organizations are both much more fulfilled when the outcomes desired dictate the hire.

Furthermore, in the church we need to be willing to engage in evaluation and training of staff while working to accomplish goals that are unified across the organization. Sometimes a job may grow beyond a person's ability to find joy in the position and to be effective for the organization. At such times we need to be willing to work to realign staff; meaning, difficult conversations need to be had and difficult decisions made.

Clearly, when boards are ineffective and staff are not in the correct roles, organizations will be mediocre at best. In order to be a vital organization, effective boards and staff are key. That is why this is the first item in the Ten Steps to Success.

SOME EXAMPLES

To illustrate the key point above, here are a few stories to think about.

- A pastor felt that a robust young adult ministry was seriously lacking in the congregation where he was recently called. The staff person responsible had little passion or expertise in reaching young adults. So, the pastor and board created a vision for a thriving young adult ministry with a vision statement of what that would look like. The staff person recognized that he was the wrong fit and took another position. Then, a talented young adult leader was brought in, and the fastest growing demographic in this congregation today is people under thirty years old.

- A council was stuck on an issue that had an $800 price tag. Some members wanted to stop what was taking place and freeze the event because it was $800 over budget, in spite of the fact that event could produce broad outreach. Nobody could find a way out of the situation until one member said, "Here is $100; if the rest of you give $50 each, or a gift according to your means, I'm confident we can have the $800 needed and just move on." *Scarcity mentality had frozen the group until someone on the council chose to lead and move the ministry forward.*

- A vestry established a budget in the fall, then held a planning retreat in January to decide what to do for the current year. It turned out this congregation rarely accomplished anything new because there was never any money to accomplish new goals. *A strategic plan gives guidance to what you should be funding and how to establish priorities.*

- A congregation identified that service to the community was a core value. However, no service to the community item was listed in their budget. "Where your treasure is, there your heart will be also" (Matt 6:21). *Leadership needs to look at who they are and if, in fact, the organization is living out that identity. If not, that organization will begin to die.*

- A congregation couldn't figure out why they were shrinking. However, they had no growth goal or even a goal for welcoming first-time visitors. How many first-time visitors did you have last year (or last month)? What is the goal for the number of first-time visitors? If the answer is "We don't know" or "We don't have a goal for this," it is likely you will not grow. We tend to be good at those things to which we pay close attention. If we have a goal for first-time visitors, we will implement tactics to achieve that goal. *It is council's job to establish and monitor the goal. A team of members of the congregation needs to take ownership of the goal to see that it is implemented.*

Once board and staff are equipped to lead the organization appropriately, then they must be equipped to lead in stewardship and fundraising. If we are going to transform the culture in our congregations to one of abundance, the key leaders—staff and board—must be actively involved in leading this transition. The pastor should not be excluded from stewardship conversations. The culture of some congregations has been to do so, or the pastor self-selects to not be present for stewardship conversations. In *Ask, Thank, Tell*, author Charles Lane makes the claim that "[sometimes] people don't want the pastor involved because as long as the spiritual/financial division is intact, then people don't have to hold their financial lives up to the light of scripture."[2] This won't lead to transformation or culture change. All it will lead to is decline.

In order for leaders to lead in the area of money, they must be willing to discern their own feelings about money. Nouwen says, "We will never be able to ask for money if we do not know how we ourselves relate to money."[3] Pastors have shared with me that they are afraid they will treat people more favorably if they know what those people give. That is not how I relate to money, so I don't understand that. I never treat anyone better for giving more, but I will treat people differently and will educate differently based on where I perceive them to be on their generosity journey.

In the congregation setting, we don't suggest setting benchmarks for how much someone must give to be in

2. Charles Lane, *Ask, Thank, Tell: Improving Stewardship Ministry in Your Congregation* (Minneapolis: Augsburg Fortress, 2006), 61.

3. Henri Nouwen, *A Spirituality of Fundraising* (Nashville: Upper Room, 2011), 27.

leadership in a congregation. I do, however, ask that anyone who leads in the area of fundraising be someone who is growing in generosity. Depending on life situations, especially during divorce or loss, sometimes people will grow in generosity, and the dollar amount of their gift will actually go down. That happens. However, as long as every leader is growing in generosity, culture will change, and they can lead the congregation to abundance.

In order to hold the leadership accountable, it is appropriate to create without names a chart such as the one below. It reflects the giving patterns of the council members and their commitment for the future. The chart may look like this:

	Year 1	Year 2	Intent for next year
Member 1	$3,000	$3,200	$4,000
Member 2	$200	$250	$900
Member 3	$12,000	$11,000	$12,500
Member 4	$875	$1,100	$2,500
Member 5	$7,000	$9,000	$8,500*

* The council member giving less overall dollars for next year is still growing in generosity due to a life situation.

In some cases, it is helpful for the leadership to discuss with the pastor where the pastor is compared to the other board members. I don't always recommend this, but in most communities, the pastor should not be in the top ten giving households. In too many congregations, the pastor is one of the top three donors to a congregation. A goal should be established that the pastor drop out of the top ten, not by decreasing their giving, but by others who have more income and assets growing in their giving.

As leaders lead, the congregation will follow. I find congregation members hungry to be led to be more effective as a church. It is critical for leaders to understand the changing dynamics of church life and recognize that we can no longer grow or thrive by being complacent. Board development takes time and energy. Discerning a vital future takes time and energy. Equipping leaders in the congregation takes intentionality and tenacity, but it is worth it. Strong leaders will lead to a vital congregation, even in today's challenging environment.

I also encourage you to perform a budget audit. Determine where your money is being invested. Does it align with your core values and who you truly are? If not, people will likely not be as generous as you hope. People give abundantly where their core values align with what is being funded by the organization.

A quality queen will lead the colony to abundance and it will thrive as everything aligns in the colony. So, too, a congregation thrives as leaders and the congregation align in where to lead the congregation into the future.

CHAPTER 3.

THE FINANCIAL STEWARDSHIP PLAN

When three weeks old, a female honeybee will leave the hive for the first time to go collect nectar or pollen. She won't just fly around and see if she can find a flower. Other bees that have been out collecting will do a dance in the hive that reflects the location of the good flowers in relationship to the sun. So, the new worker will immediately know where to go to find a quality nectar or pollen source. They have a plan and follow the plan. At the same time, a smaller percentage of the bees will be out looking for the next great pollen or nectar source. Part of their plan is looking for new resources to replace what will inevitably run out someday.

It is amazing how many churches and organizations don't actually have a financial development plan. There are a number of reasons for this. In the church, we pass the plates each week and assume people will be as generous as they are capable of being. If we become desperate, we will send a letter requesting additional gifts or ask a couple of wealthy people to bail us out. We assume everyone knows the theological and biblical reasons to give. We assume people have been taught to be good stewards and have modeled generosity throughout their lives. We assume way too much. We need to have a strategy and build a plan. Without such a plan, people simply see us asking and asking without any cultivation of the spirituality of abundance. This leaves donors thinking we just want their money.

PUTTING A PLAN IN PLACE

Deliberate activity is critical. Certain areas or steps cannot be overlooked.

DATA

I haven't found church-management or donor software that I truly love. For me, these tools simply offer different levels of satisfaction. However, I do like donor software better than simply using Excel or 3″ × 5″ index cards to record giving. Effective stewardship efforts must do an effective job of managing data so we know who is giving to us, how much and how often they are giving, and to what appeals people are responding.

As I'm writing this, a congregation reported to me that they don't have the 147 families they thought they did; they actually have eighty-five. Of course, this huge difference will make a difference in the size of the "asks" in order to reach a goal. Managing data well is essential in order to know who should be supporting your ministry and mission. Congregations also need people who are excellent at managing data and understanding the data management system. With online training, YouTube videos, and tech support, it is easy today to be excellent at keeping up with data. You will also find there are people in your congregation who find great joy in managing and analyzing data. It is a gift to them to let them thrive in the stewardship function of data management.

MAIL

In order to be effective, mailed messages must be augmented by social media, email, and other digital means and repeated if you expect it to drive robust results. Sending out four pieces of mail per year is not a stewardship or fundraising plan. I have seen congregations behind on their budget send a letter and conclude that they have fixed everything by this one tactic. In the nonprofit world, a 10 percent response rate to such a letter is seen as excellent. So, by sending one letter you might, if you are really fortunate, get a response from 10 percent of your donors. Having said this, mail is by no means dead, even for younger families. Younger families may respond differently than older generations, but they still respond well to mail. What we find is that younger donors will read your mail but make their gift on your website or social media page. Older donors are more likely to write a check. I suggest sending an e-blast a couple days after the letter and include in the blast a link to the giving option on the church website. This will help maximize the direct mail response. If all you do is send a piece of mail, don't be surprised if the response rate is not as high as you hoped it would be. The fault may not lie with your list of families but with your plan.

CASE

Solid fundraising work flows out of a strong case for gifts. When I started as a fundraiser, I was sent to a class called "Principles and Techniques of Fundraising" at what is now the Lilly Family School of Philanthropy. It was a five-day class, and I think the entire first day was about case development. If you cannot articulate what people should give to, you won't raise any money. Here's an import tip: Avoid falling into the trap of thinking your case is your organization. Your case is how your organization impacts the world, but not the organization itself. Never say, "You should give to "Best Christian Ministries." Instead, say, "Your gift to Best Christian Ministries will provide what is needed to help us change the world." Articulate what that life-changing ministry is that you do.

Three questions are helpful as you seek to build your case.

- *So what?* What is the unmet human need the congregation has identified and believes it is called to address? What is the congregation's reason for being?

- *Who cares?* Who will benefit from the congregation's response, and how will they benefit?

- *Why you?* What makes this congregation especially suited to carry on the work envisioned?

PUBLIC RELATIONS

How do you tell your church's story? Does the story that is told align with what the invitation states the donations will support? Both churches and other institutions should also ask if the story is only for people who already know you. If so, it is likely new people will not be reached. The storytelling may need to be segmented for the different audiences one is trying to reach.

When creating an annual development plan, consider the following:

- *Case.* What is our case for support? Why should people give to our organization? How will their gifts expand the kingdom of God?

- *Annual fund.* What is the dollar goal? How many donors do we expect to contribute? How will we approach them for their gift? Can we ask more than once and for more than one item? How do we renew gifts? How do we find new donors?

- *Capital fund.* You won't always have this, but when you do, it requires significant volunteer engagement, a clear and compelling case, and a direct ask that allows everyone to know how critical their support is.

- *Planned giving.* This is often the most ignored part of any development plan, whether a church or institution. I often ask congregation leaders how many funerals they had last year, and of those who died, how many included the congregation in their estate plans. This will demonstrate how well the congregation's planned giving program is working.

A DEVELOPMENT PLAN

So, what does a development plan for the annual fund of a congregation look like?

Trinity Church
Stewardship Development Calendar
Annual Giving

Date of this calendar:

	Yr. 1 Sept	Oct	Nov	Dec	Yr. 2 Jan	Feb	March	April	May	June	July	Aug	Sept	Oct	Nov	Dec
1. Annual Appeal for Statement of Intents		X	X	X										X	X	X
2. Bible Studies						x	x									
3. Giving report and reminder				X		X			X			X				X
4. Newsletter articles, website, emails, social media																
5. Special Gift Appeal letters						X	X									
6. Sermons on stewardship	X					X			X			X				
7. New members																
8. New Donors/ Visitors																
9. Trinity Stories	X X	X X	X X	X X	X X	X X	X X	X X	X X	X X	X X	X X	X X	X X	X X	X X
10. Major Donors																

The numbering of these statements coincides to the numbers on the Annual Stewardship Calendar.

1. **Annual appeal for statement of intent:** This is the ongoing stewardship appeal effort usually conducted in the fall. Congregations should be doubling revenues every seven years. It is critical to have people complete a statement of intents because it is

through intentional giving that people are able to be much more generous. You should conduct the appeal when you can reach the most people. A gift of $1 per day would cause many "random" donors to double their giving or better. In *Passing the Plate*, studies found that Lutherans who pledged gave 45 percent more than nonpledging Lutherans; pledging Catholics gave 77 percent more than nonpledging Catholics; and pledging Baptists gave 34 percent more than nonpledging Baptists.[1]

2. **Bible studies and generosity story sharing:** At least once during the calendar year, some form of Bible study or generosity story sharing should take place to help the congregation grow in their understanding of their relationship with their possessions. These can be segmented to small groups or conducted congregation-wide.

3. **Giving reports and reminders:** Timely, accurate, and pertinent information should be sent out on a regular basis to the congregation. These should be upbeat and exciting, and even contain outcome stories of what God is doing through the ministry. My preference is to send these out in the following schedule.

1. Christian Smith, Michael O. Emerson, and Patricia Snell, *Passing the Plate: Why American Christians Don't Give Away More Money* (Oxford: Oxford University Press, 2008), 95.

a. January 31: This date helps you monitor if people have adjusted their giving for the new year and remind people what you plan to accomplish.

b. April 30: This report will always include Easter giving, so the comparison to previous years will always be an accurate comparison to the ebbs and flows of church attendance.

c. August 31: This is a great time for people to reflect on giving as they come back from the summer vacation schedule and programs relaunch at the church.

d. November 30: This allows you to capture year-end giving.

Whether your fiscal year is the calendar year or aligns with the academic calendar, these dates are designed to stimulate giving from the perspective of when donors are most ready to give. One caveat is that if you have a June 30 year end, it is possible to send a May 31 letter about the urgency of finishing the fiscal year strong and fully funding all your ministries.

4. **Newsletter articles:** Focus on thanking people for generosity, sharing outcome stories of what financial gifts are helping to accomplish, and sharing stewardship principles. This can also be a place for people to share their own generosity stories.

5. **Special gift appeal:** Once a year, conduct a special gift appeal for a specific ministry not covered by

the annual fund. This helps people to give some of their discretionary money to causes dear to them. It is also a tool used to help grow donors from the mid-level to becoming more generous. Often, it takes a clear, concise project that someone is passionate about to help them grow to a new level of giving.

6. **Sermons on stewardship:** Sermons emphasizing God's generosity to us and our grateful response through being generous should happen throughout the year. People are sometimes more apt to be open to these sermons when they are being delivered outside appeal season.

7. **New members:** Present your stewardship ministry perspective at one of the new member classes. Be sure to educate and also inspire. As people are joining the church, they should be at their greatest openness to being challenged to generosity because they are choosing to be part of your ministry and want it to thrive. If you want to change culture in the area of stewardship, start with your new members. They are not aware yet of some of the "normal" or traditional patterns of giving in your congregation. Start changing behavior with this group, and eventually it will permeate across the congregation.

8. **New donors/visitors:** Every time a gift is received from a nonmember, send a personal letter thanking them. Include a handwritten signature. If someone gives to the congregation who is not a member, they are stating that they care about the organization and want to get to know it better.

9. **Stories:** These are simply stories, reports, and observations on what is being accomplished by the congregation's activities and thus by the generous giving of the people. These stories are a great way to encourage the congregation and help avoid staff and volunteer burnout, because they remind us why the ministry is so valuable. Stories get at the heart of what impact our ministry has on people's lives.

10. **Major donors:** Prepare a plan of action for major donors. Design a personal strategy for cultivating and growing these donors toward more significant support of your ministry. Make room for major donor activities and visits on your calendar. You don't need to treat these people more favorably than anyone else, but you can treat them differently to grow their support of your ministry. Some of the most effective work with major donors comes in periods of time between stewardship drives, when you are not asking for money. Focus on seeking to engage these donors more deeply in the ministry of the congregation.

Abundance is achieved when we have a plan and we work it. It does not happen by accident. Just as the new bee leaving the colony does not leave the colony to find nectar and pollen by accident, so too our people grow in generosity.

CHAPTER 4.

STRATEGIC VISION

Honeybees are very focused on their mission. The mission is that the colony survives. The vision is that the species expands and thrives. The core values are that the home is sacred and will be defended, and that each worker will do their job until they move to the next job, or die in the process. In support of this mission, they often have just two goals. The first goal is to store up enough honey to make it through the winter without starving to death when there is no nectar to be found. The second goal happens when there is an abundance of nectar. They split themselves and allow the old queen and half the hive to swarm to a new location. Instead of one hive, there will be two hives with a new queen taking over the original hive to carry on the mission as two colonies instead of one. I really wish our churches would follow this mentality more often!

When bees experience abundance, they start another colony. A pastor I was working with called me one day and said, "Well, it happened." A donor had walked into her office and said, "What would you do with $10,000?" She had no answer. Fortunately, she was able to stall until after we talked, and she came up with a plan. If we don't have an idea what might be done with an extra $10,000, our donors may ensure that we never receive an extra

$10,000! In this chapter we will talk about how to plan strategically, to be prepared for when abundance knocks at our door unexpectedly, and how to plan so that abundance naturally occurs.

PEOPLE GIVE TO A VISION

Congregations often grow significantly (10–30 percent) in their first year working with GSB on their annual stewardship. But growth in the second and subsequent years requires a robust strategic plan that adequately defines what opportunities the congregation wants to pursue next. People give to vision. The reason colleges and hospitals get million-dollar gifts is that they have million-dollar visions. Congregations and church institutions will receive these gifts when their vision for impacting the world for the kingdom of God demands these types of gifts. The same is true with $10,000 and $1,000 gifts. Without a vision, you will rarely receive extra money. Vision helps your organization move beyond survival to thriving.

Strong vision is never more important than at the end of the fiscal year. Many congregations and institutions ask for year-end help to balance the budget. Honestly, most donors don't care about balanced budgets unless they serve on the finance committee. They care about impact. They care about the ministry's vision of what is planned to make a difference in the world through financial gifts. When you focus on this vision in a specific manner, generosity will become a part of the congregation's experience. Stating what you will do with revenue that exceeds expenses is a great way to show donors that you have plans beyond a balanced budget.

I recall hearing John Maxwell say at a conference that we fail to dream "God-sized dreams" in the church. We allow scarcity mentality to keep us from thinking we can try new stuff and move beyond the status quo. This lets scarcity thinking win. I had a donor who was very excited to give $25,000 to $50,000 per year to try new efforts in marketing for our outdoor ministry. His only requirement was that we learned from what we tried, but he also desperately wanted us to thrive and reach more people. He knew that pulling back would not allow us to have a robust future. He freed us to dream. You cannot cut your way to abundance. I have to tell you, I failed a lot! However, during that time we doubled our revenue from nonsummer guests because we had the freedom to see what would work. We began to dream God-sized dreams. In this case, the donor helped us have the vision. More donors than we realize are waiting for us to have a vision and to invite them to participate in that vision.

I also hear people say that they get "fatigued" being asked for money. My experience is that is not what is going on. People get "fatigued" when they don't see their increased giving leading to significant, new, or enhanced ministry. Too often in the church we think we need new tactics to raise money. Changing tactics may help once in a while, but strong focus on expanding the vision that is being implemented is what gets people excited. People want to make a difference in the world. They will give more money to make that happen, but they need to have confidence that the plan is strategic, thoughtful, and attainable. They need to feel that more than just surviving is at stake. Donor fatigue is also a symptom of failing to inspire, which I will address later.

In my first call, the church had a long-standing tradition of adopting a budget in November, followed by a planning retreat in January. You guessed it—we weren't being very strategic or creative, and we certainly were not dreaming "God-sized dreams" because we had no money to implement anything creative. We had the cart before the horse. Our planning was, in a sense, limited by our budget. We needed to be building the budget according to our visionary planning.

BUILDING A STRATEGIC PLAN

So, what does a strategic plan look like? There are so many models out there, I understand how it is possible to be confused on what a strategic plan truly looks like. For me, the strategic plan needs to include two parts:

1. A description of institutional identity
2. A statement of goals illustrating how you will live out that identity

Strategic plans are grounded in an understanding of institutional identity, which includes mission, vision, and core values. Some planners like to include purpose statements and other language. That is fine, but mission, vision, and core values are the basics of identity. Then, to live out as well as expand and enhance identity, we define goals, objectives, and tactics.

Having an understanding of who we are as an organization is critical to know what we are to do. A congregation in Bastrop, Texas, with an average worship attendance of forty people discerned their mission needed to be intimately connected to education. So, they chose to develop a preeminent preschool that is now thriving, provides significant ministry value to the community, and gives the members of the congregation a sense of making an impact for the kingdom of God.

Mission defines who we are, and therefore what we don't do. It defines our purpose in the world. If done well, it allows people to know what they will find if they choose to be part of the organization. If we give it some thought, our mission statement can free us to become what the world needs us to become. Too often, mission statements are too long, churchy, and trite. Don't just string a bunch of church words or core activities together. A mission statement of "We worship, learn, serve, and care" is not a mission statement but instead a list of what you do. Define why you exist, and state it clearly in as few words as possible.

Some examples of mission statements that completely define congregations include:

- "Equip all to be the heart, hands, and feet of Jesus in the world" (Abiding Hope Lutheran Church, Littleton, Colorado)

- "Connecting people through Christ and community" (Abiding Presence Lutheran Church, Burke, Virginia)

I'm currently reading *Canoeing the Mountains*, in which author Tod Bolsinger discusses the need for a mission statement of conviction. He lays out a process for developing a mission statement based on one developed by the Mulago Foundation. The statement must be in the following format: *Verb, target, outcome*.

Not only must it follow that format, but it also must be just eight words. Bolsinger shares that some of his clients have developed mission statements such as the following.

- Nurture our congregation for deployment in Christ's kingdom

- Prepare all generations to impact lives for Christ

He states, "These are not generic statements. They are specific to each organization." He goes on to share that the discussion around each and limiting the statement to eight words leads to conviction that it truly represents what the organization is about.[1]

In addition to stating who you are, a solid mission statement also tells the world what you are not. Mission creep is dangerous for an organization, and churches are susceptible to it. Mission creep happens when we start chasing fads or launching programs where we have no expertise or competency and thus take critical resources away from our actual mission. The challenge here is that not all churches have the same mission. So, a church in another town may have a wonderful after-school tutoring program that is making a huge impact on children in the community. If your mission has nothing to do with educating children, your congregation should not just launch a program like this. It is great ministry, it just doesn't fit your congregation. Most often, congregations fall into mission creep when they recognize a weakness in their own ministry and just start dreaming up things to do to fix the weakness. Sometimes it is okay to simply say, "We don't do that here, but if that is important to you, we can help you find a church that offers that particular ministry."

Vision is what we see the world becoming when we live out our mission. Too often, our vision is small and reflects

1. Tod Bolsinger, *Canoeing the Mountains: Christian Leadership in Uncharted Territory* (Downers Grove, IL: InterVarsity, 2015), 132–33.

a scarcity mindset. Habitat for Humanity has a vision of "a world where everyone has a decent place to live." I pray that someday this vision becomes reality. It is bold and courageous and assumes abundance. Churches need to have visions like "Everyone understands they are loved by God," or "Everyone experiences sabbath rest," or "Faith is passed among all generations." I'm not here to tell you what your vision should be, but I do want to encourage you to articulate your vision and live it out like you believe you can accomplish it. Vision is what makes us go to work every day as we live out our mission. We see what the world can become, and we become passionate to see that come about. If our vision is simply that we won't close our doors, we will eventually get tired enough that we don't care. Vision can keep us going even when things become difficult. Without much question, it is harder to be church today than it was back in the 1970s and 1980s. Vision helps us work through the rough moments and believe in a day when engagement in our mission is more robust than it ever has been and that our world needs what we offer now more than ever.

Core values are what really set us apart as congregations. You may have many values, but in my opinion you cannot have more than four core values. After four, they may describe your values, but they are no longer core. Core values are those values that if they are not tended to within your system, conflict will result. For example, when two congregations merge, if they understand each other's core values, they can find a way to live together. If they don't, they will fight with one another. The congregation in which I grew up thought one of its core values was to reach new people for Christ. But they had not really been living out this value. They called a pastor who shared that core value. He was more interested in new people than nurturing the people who were already there. He wasn't a bad pastor. He is what they asked for. It turned out that his priorities differed from those of the congregation. Though the new people that came into the church loved him, he lasted less than a couple of years before the tension over these core values was too high.

Those who had been at this congregation for some time actually had a core value of community and compassion for one another. That core value was not nurtured and therefore led to conflict in the congregation. Each congregation or organization has many values, but only four of them can be "core." Define them. Be honest about them. Then, robustly live into them!

The better you identify your core values, the better you will know how to motivate your congregation. If you have ever tried to launch a new program and nobody came, it is likely that it didn't align with people's core values. For example, a congregation once cancelled worship on Sunday morning to go serve the community. That sounds like a good idea, except that worship was far and away this congregation's number one core value. Though service in the community was an aspiration for many, it wasn't a core value in this congregation. This caused some consternation. Rather than cancelling worship altogether, perhaps worship could have been held and then paused in order to engage in a service project, or perhaps the project could have been launched right after the service. Or worship could have been conducted right in the midst of the service project. Working against your core values leads to conflict and disappointment. Utilizing them to advance the ministry can help the organization function much more smoothly with higher levels of engagement.

A great example of using your core values to lead into your aspirations is a congregation whose leadership wanted more community engagement, but that was not a core value of the congregation. In this congregation, family ministry is recognized as most sacred. Therefore, leadership began to plan family service opportunities in the community. These were well attended and appreciated because it nurtured the core value of family ministry.

The most effective organizations and churches are those who know who they are and seek to live into that rather than trying to be something they are not. They don't chase fads. They continue to work to become better at being who they really are.

ESTABLISHING SMART GOALS

Once you know your organizational identity, you are ready to establish goals for living into this identity. Goals can be long-term and somewhat aspirational. The best goals are SMART goals:

- **S**pecific
- **M**easurable
- **A**chievable
- **R**elevant
- **T**imely

Tactics are tools to make goals a reality. Unfortunately, in the church, we often confuse goals and tactics. *What people truly want to fund through their financial support are goals, but too often we ask people to support tactics.* Please underline and highlight that last statement as it could be the biggest error that gets repeated in our churches, and it hinders generosity and abundance. The best tactics are meaningless without clearly stated and robust goals. I repeat: what people want to fund through their financial support are goals, but too often we lead with tactics.

Many congregations say that they need a youth director or associate pastor. Both of these items should be tactics in order to reach a bigger goal. We should start with the goal and then invite people to help make the tactic a reality for the sake of the goal. So, start with a goal such as, "We desire our children and youth to be able to have faith and articulate it in a way that can carry them through life's challenges." In order to reach this goal, we need to hire a youth director (tactic). Or, "Our goal is to welcome everyone who passes through our doors with a feeling that they are welcomed as Christ welcomes any stranger." Therefore, we need to replace the roof (tactic) so that guests to our congregation don't get wet inside our classrooms when it is raining outside. Roofs, buildings, and staff members are not goals. They are tactics to reach goals that help us live into our mission and reach the vision we have for advancing the kingdom of God in the world.

Objectives are helpful when a goal is complex enough that it requires an aligned process to accomplish the goal. The examples provided in appendix C demonstrate what I am referring to here. If a goal is robust enough, it will require several objectives in order to accomplish, and then many tactics to accomplish each objective.

We focus on the strategic plan in order to set the stage for robust stewardship and fundraising because failure to develop our vision for the future will result in donors who are not excited about supporting our ministry. Don't create what I would call a "list of stuff" and present it during the stewardship drive. This reads like a laundry list of items with price tags associated with each (e.g., health insurance—$6,000; parking lot paving—$20,000; salary increases—$1,200). It feels like paying bills and doesn't make people feel like you are preparing for anything significant or honoring the ministry impact of each of these items. Donors see right through this. If our projects don't align with a larger vision and goal for impacting the future, donors will feel that we are just after money, and they won't respond in a generous manner. Furthermore, people in the church have a great ability to argue with tactics that are not attached to a larger goal. It is hard to argue with a robust goal that aligns with our identity. On the other hand, it is easy to argue the value of a tactic that doesn't seem to have any bigger purpose or connection to our vision. For instance, I may be inclined to say, "We don't need a youth director because the parents can simply lead the activities." But, if we state a goal of "our youth being able to have faith and articulate it in a way that can carry them through life's challenges," I quickly recognize that a professional youth director is needed to help make that a reality, and I would never argue against youth having this type of faith.

I have heard congregations talk about strategic planning done a few years ago, but those plans are on a shelf gathering dust. That can happen when the plan doesn't have a clear vision and is not based around SMART goals. A strategic plan that is simply a listing of a lot of tactics is doomed to fail. One congregation I worked with handed me their old plan and said, "We didn't really accomplish much of this." When I read it, I wasn't surprised. It was a list of thirty-nine tactics, including that the secretary should learn to use Excel. I don't disagree that the secretary should learn Excel, but that is not a goal. It could be a tactic, but in the context of a list of thirty-nine tactics, it just felt busy.

Organize the strategic plan around three or four goals that help the vision for the congregation become a reality. A plan done this way is bound to be successful and lead to a congregation that is vital and full of life. And this congregation will be better positioned to attain significant financial support.

My internship was at Christ Lutheran in Wise, Virginia. This is a congregation with an average worship attendance of less than thirty per week. Before my arrival, they identified themselves as an educating congregation and had developed a tutoring program for the community. This program led to growth and purpose for this small congregation.

Just as a strong honeybee colony rallies around its mission, people in Wise rallied around their mission, and they experienced growth and purpose. A quality strategic plan leads to purpose and growth in all settings.

PART II.

EXPANDING THE FUNDRAISING PLAN

We believe that the annual fund of a congregation or organization can be doubled every five to seven years as long as the organization understands its identity and has a vision worthy of that plan. The doubling doesn't happen by all donors doubling their gift during that period. Some will grow by far more than that amount. However, when strong identity and vision exist, and as the organization has an impact, many more will join the effort. In fact, if congregations do this well, the storytelling that results from stewardship and fundraising can lead to an organic witness in the world.

CHAPTER 5.

CASE DEVELOPMENT

When a honeybee colony decides it is going to split, there are a number of decisions made. As soon as half the colony departs the hive with the old queen, they will settle down and cluster on a branch or mailbox or some other surface usually just a few yards from the old hive. They often look like a football while all gathered there. While clustered, scout bees leave the other bees who are protecting the queen to go find a suitable new home. Upon finding a potential new location in a hollow tree, a dryer vent, or the eaves of a house, the scout bee will return to the cluster and do a dance to tell the other bees about what she has found. If she is convincing, a few other scout bees will go with her to the location to discern if they approve. Then, they return. However, by this time, other scout bees have returned with other suitable locations. The bees that give the best dance and make the best case for why their location is the most suitable for the colony will ultimately convince the colony where to settle. The bees who make the most compelling case for their location ultimately sway the hive's choice of new residence.

Your congregation or organization is not the only non-profit competing for the philanthropic support of your members. You have to make the case for how your organization and your goals will have the greatest impact on the world and connect with your donors' passions. Back when I took Principles and Techniques of Fundraising from what is now the Lilly Family School of Philanthropy, we learned that the case is "a clear, compelling statement justifying the request for funds." The case is not your organization; it is what your organization will do with funds to advance its mission.

In the past, making the case for support was pretty simple: "We are the church, and you should support us." That seemed to work fine when the church was one of the centers of the cultural universe. People supported churches simply because it was the thing to do. Churches seemed to have plenty of money not only to survive but also to expand.

This model isn't effective anymore. Trying to raise money in this way is out of touch with reality. We owe our donors more than that. We need to develop our case. As leaders, we are also more fulfilled when we clearly articulate why we exist, how we impact the world, and how we are seeking to grow our impact.

Our *case* demonstrates why a gift to our organization is important. It demonstrates urgency. It demonstrates impact. Our case is not the mortgage, the personnel line in the budget, or the budget itself. Our case is telling people how a gift to our organization will impact the kingdom of God now.

One recent trend in congregations is to move to a case of funding social service opportunities within the church. Sometimes the case is even stated as, "Give more to us so we can give more away." As I said in an earlier chapter, I agree that Jesus told his followers to feed the hungry, clothe the naked, visit the prisoner, and more. We should do these things. I think we have moved to this social ministry case because it is tangible. But I also believe we can make a good case for pastoral care, worship, faith development, and Christian community and show them to be tangible as well. Making worship and pastoral care tangible outcomes of our case development takes time and is difficult work, especially if it involves more intimate sharing, however it is incredibly rewarding to be part of these ministries.

If your organization asks for more dollars so more can be given away, you must be prepared to demonstrate why it is more important to give through your church than directly to the receiving organization. If we cannot do that, the donor will ask why they shouldn't just support that organization directly and perhaps diminish support of the congregation.

Here is an example of making the case for pastoral care. My daughter's best friend was killed on Good Friday a few years ago by a drunk driver who was going the wrong way on the interstate. It was tragic, and I can still feel the pain that my daughter was going through as I witnessed her receive the call that brought her the devastating news. There were no words to make it better. No magic formula for what to do. My daughter was in tremendous emotional pain. However, in the midst of a very busy couple of days for the church, our pastor dropped everything and gave Caroline the time and care she needed. Pastor Rachel cared for her as only a pastor could and delivered some comfort and good news in the midst of a true Good Friday experience.

At that moment, I came to fully understand the value of pastoral care as a tangible action of the church, but I couldn't understand why we as a church don't promote pastoral care as a portion of the case for financial support.

As I have reflected on this, I think it is because we forget to ask recipients of pastoral care to talk publicly about their experience. Doing so is too intimate and takes too much energy to get the story. In our congregation reporting, we boil these stories down to "the pastor made six hospital visits this week." That number actually means little on its own. We need to hear the story, the outcome, of the person whose life began to become whole again and felt God's presence brought to the situation through pastoral care. Those of us who have received or given pastoral care will fully understand the impact and be delighted to give financially to make certain that all who are part of our Christian community receive that type of quality pastoral care. However, if we never talk about the impact, we can forget the value of it; many people will forget that this provides such an incredible need to the people we love and care for.

In my opinion, we also seem to undervalue the importance of worship in our lives by not making the opportunity to worship the center of our stewardship case. Most congregations look to tangible facility improvements or social ministry activities but seldom emphasize weekly worship as they ask for money. If we don't invest more in our worship experience, we likely won't be able to improve the experience to reach more people. New types of music, artwork, drama, guest preachers, sound systems, paint, carpet, and more can all enhance worship. It makes me wonder why we often focus on what is not the center of our life together. I think it is because it is easier to talk about facilities and outreach. They are seen as more urgent.

I believe worship is the most critical opportunity that our churches offer the world, because it is in worship that people can experience sabbath rest and God's presence in the midst of our chaotic lives. In worship we recognize that we are not God, and our burdens can be shared with the One who is. We need to articulate this to help people see their need for worship and to financially support what is critical to our faith journey. And we need to recognize that giving itself is as an act of worship. As we do, we also remind people of why we worship, and they can become compelled to invite others to worship to receive this opportunity as well.

As we develop our case for support, we need to reflect deeply on the core ministry that we do and make that relevant to our people. By doing this well, we will all find our ministry more engaging and relevant to their lives.

The scout bees in a honeybee colony are all about the survival and positioning of the colony to thrive in the future. When they return to the hive, they demonstrate their case in the most compelling manner possible. In the church setting, we need to make our case urgent and compelling for our audience as well. Whether your case is based on tried-and-true ministry, such as strong pastoral care and meaning-filled worship, or highlighting new ministry possibilities that keep the congregation's eyes on the future, take time to discern and present your case. A strong case presented in a compelling way leads to donors who are excited to support ministry and be engaged in it. We have the story of God, who is active and involved in our world, which should provide for the most compelling case that our people hear.

So, how do we present this case to our donors and supporters? Fortunately, we don't have to come back to the church and do a dance! We can tell our story in a positive, exciting, and uplifting manner that leads people to believe that our best days of ministry are in front of us. We teach that you can do that best by downplaying the overall money needed and instead focus on what you will do with net new money that you receive from people. Furthermore, this will help people to feel less overwhelmed by the total money needed, and instead they can focus on what can be accomplished as they increase their giving. The best cases are those that paint a picture of how life in the congregation and surrounding community will be enhanced by the work that is being funded. The case should also be tangible and one that people can easily wrap their mind around.

Case development is a concept that is well understood among nonprofit organizations. An example case I recently developed for a middle judicatory is as follows.

In 2020, we need to have a net increase in Mission Support of $8,333 per month. With this increase, we will add the following to our story:

- An additional $20,000 investment in our camping ministries as they continue to raise up leaders and pass on faith.

- An expanded ministry and presence with congregations pursuing shared ministry arrangements such as yoking or anchor agreements.

- A $15,000 investment in the creation of a holistic Ending Well ministry focused on supporting rostered ministers nearing or entering retirement.

- Funds to provide a coach for all rostered ministers taking a new call for the first year of that transition.

This case is effective because it doesn't show everything the organization will do with every dollar received. It focuses on how much they need over what they have received in the past and what tangible outcomes they seek with those increased gifts. These outcomes were tested with the constituency, and most of the supporters will resonate with and feel passion for at least one of the initiatives.

These same case-development principles relate to congregational life. Seek to develop a case for support that is tangible and exciting for your congregation, and your members and supporters will be much more inclined to consider increasing their financial support. They will know why their increased giving is so important. We need to do the same for the congregation that was done for the middle judicatory.

CHAPTER 6.

COMMUNICATION FOR WHEN YOU ARE ASKING AND WHEN YOU AREN'T

By simply releasing a scent, honeybees can communicate. The queen releases a pheromone that spreads to all the other bees in the colony. Guard bees wait at the entrance to smell returning foragers to make sure they are returning to their own hive and aren't actually robber bees coming to steal honey. Other pheromones are released by control bees who keep up with how much pollen and nectar is coming into the hive, and they give the order for the queen to be fed more to lay more eggs to expand the colony. Or they see a dearth and give the order for her to be fed less and create fewer new bees. If a bear or person attacks the hive, the bees release an alarm pheromone that gets left on the attacker so that all the other bees know who to sting! All the communication flows through the queen. Queenless hives don't communicate well, and if you look at them, they are in disarray as they die a slow death.

Just about every congregation I visit says something like, "If we just fix our communications, more people will participate, join us, or be engaged with our ministry." Some think hiring someone to concentrate on communications is the answer. Others think creating a Facebook page or Twitter account is the answer. Others use the strategy of placing advertisements on different social media and search engines.

The problem for most congregations is not *how* but rather *what* they communicate. I encourage you to read that sentence again! Actually, I will just repeat it. The problem for most congregations is not *how* but rather *what* they communicate.

My favorite activity when coaching congregations on annual stewardship is to conduct a communications audit. Many find it odd that I spend so much time on communication. But whenever we produce a bulletin or newsletter that is read by our donors, it is a donor communication. We need to evaluate the message our donors hear year round, because when we come to ask them for money, all those communications will inform their perception of the ministry and its ability to handle generous gifts.

I have mentioned previously one of my least favorite forms of communication in church. Many congregations publish what I call the box score in the bulletin each week.

Offering last week: $8,400
Offering needed: $9,600
Shortfall: $1,200

There it is for all the world to see in our bulletin each week. A message to all our donors that we aren't doing enough. We fall short. If you are one of the people who gave more money last week than you have ever given before, you will feel like you are alone. You are alone in your generosity, so you might as well stop giving now. If you are a visitor, you won't want to stick around because they don't have enough money to operate. Get out now!

What bothers me even more about this communication

is that it often isn't true. Many congregations declare that their need is 1/52 per week as if giving is equal across all weeks. It never is and likely never will be, so stop expecting it. Approximately 35 percent of giving happens in the United States between Thanksgiving and New Year's. So, we aren't actually behind most of the calendar year.

The primary reasons I counsel against publishing the box score are the following.

- It tells us nothing of the impact any money given has made.

- There are too many variables in how people give for it to be completely accurate.

- It reinforces the idea that the budget is the goal of our giving when in reality there is much more we can do to advance the kingdom than what is in our budget.

Should we give our members an update of giving? Absolutely! But it should be in the context of impact on the world and reaching our ministry goals. It has to be done in a manner that reinforces abundance and impact.

A COMMUNICATION PLAN

Communication also needs to be targeted and not treat everyone the same. I once had a pastor say corporately, "The congregation is behind in giving." Well, that wasn't true for my family. Our bank mails a check to the church the fifteenth of every month and has never missed a single payment, although once I did forget to increase the amount when we increased our intent. We were not behind on our giving. I not only resented the remark, but it made me wonder why we should continue to grow in our giving if others around me seemed to be so lazy in their generosity.

We need to communicate strategically. I like to look at four different types of communication.

INFORMATION

We must communicate information, but let's communicate exciting information. Let's also be careful that when we share information, we lead with the right headline. Which article do you want to read: "Food pantry needs your help this Saturday!" or "I recognize the face of hunger in my neighborhood"?

You may be tempted to say that the first is more exciting because of the exclamation point that I added. But it doesn't speak to human need the way the second one does. When such needs are identified, people may actually change their behavior and come help. Punctuation, boldface type, and all caps do not communicate excitement. Content communicates excitement. Outcome communicates excitement.

INSPIRATION

This is hard to accomplish in written communication, but I have seen it done effectively. Normally it happens when people share something of themselves, often something a little more personal. Inspiration is enhanced through live interaction or video. It is so hard to get a sense of excitement or passion through written communication. We must inspire, or people will be left thinking we simply want their money or their time.

I believe outcome stories are needed for communication to have a true impact. I care less about what you did and much more about the impact it had on the people who were engaged in either delivering or receiving the ministry.

That a pastor made fourteen hospital visits last month is important, but hearing the number alone is not nearly as inspiring as hearing the stories of impact that pastoral care had on a member or nonmember of the congregation. For example, what does it mean to the spiritual healing of the person to be visited on the six-month anniversary of her husband's death? Hearing stories of pastoral care make ministry tangible. They make me feel like the church is having an impact on people's lives, so I want to share this news with my neighbor.

Listing the number of people who volunteer in worship leadership is fine, but my heart is warmed to hear the story of the person who shares that they experience God's presence in their lives most clearly when they are helping in some way with worship. It will also lead to more people wanting to participate.

I am glad to know that fourteen youth went on a mission trip, but I am more inspired to know how God worked through the experience to help their faith grow. I'm glad to hear about people making forty-five quilts for those in need, but hearing how those quilts had an impact, perhaps even saved a life, makes me more invested in the ministry. If I hear a story about someone who received a quilt having a new sense that they are loved as Christ loves all of us, the story has a real impact on me. I am happy to know our church provides space for AA, but even more, I would love to know that people who found their way to our church feel that those meetings have saved their lives as they journey to sobriety.

Tell outcome stories. Tell them all the time. Tell them as you pass the offering plates. Tell them as you gather in small groups. Start your council meetings with these stories and then share them with the congregation.

Telling our friends that our church packed fourteen backpacks this week for hungry children is important, but if we can share that a parent reported that their child has improved their grades because suddenly he or she isn't focused on an empty stomach, that is a powerful outcome story.

What we communicate matters. Nothing is more important than the impact of what we do has in the name of Jesus. I do know that this communication is hard. It is easier to post dates or other data than to discover the stories of impact. What I will tell you is that fewer people will burn out on their work in the church if we focus on impact instead of activity. Activity can be exhausting when we forget the purpose of that activity. When we realize lives are being touched with God's love and it is making a difference, the activity isn't so burdensome.

ASK

I believe our communication should always include an ask, but not necessarily an ask for money. Sometimes, we ask for volunteers, opinions, recommendations, ideas, or feedback. When people are asked to respond, they interact with the communication piece differently.

Inviting people to provide the names of three people that they think would be good to serve on altar guild, that is, allowing them to self-nominate, will cause them to hear the call from the altar guild for assistance in a different way. Asking people their opinion about the core values of the congregation will require people to think about what those core values are. Asking people to share a story of how volunteering at the food pantry has been important to their family will cause them to think differently about the article describing the needs of the food pantry. People should be in the habit of being asked to respond when we communicate with them. After all, we want people to respond when we ask them to complete their statement of intent and to make a gift.

THANK

I grew up with Jim and Tammy Faye Bakker manipulating people to give money to their "church" and then misappropriating funds. I have never been part of asking for money for a ministry that had a misappropriation of funds, but every ministry has had to deal with the Bakkers's abuse of their positions.

Because other nonprofits haven't been wholly ethical, we all must accomplish two things in our thank you. We owe our donors *gratitude* and *accountability*. Gratitude is just a healthy human trait. I once had a pastor write a personal thank-you note on the bottom of our yearly giving statement, and I remember how good it made me feel. I felt like our gifts to the church were important, and I appreciated knowing that someone cared enough to tell me that. The church needs the hearts of our members. I remind you of what Jesus says in Matthew 6:21: "Where your treasure is, there your hearts will be also." We need people to invest so we can get their heart. Let's be grateful for that piece of their heart. Let's tell people we noticed and that it matters to us that they support our work together.

Accountability is the other part of our thanks. Through saying thank you, we can tell our donors we used their gift in the way we told them we would. Furthermore, we can let people know what we accomplished, or at least what we learned from utilizing their gift for the project we undertook. I have discovered that donors don't mind you using their money for something that doesn't work if you can communicate what you learned from it and won't continue to waste their money.

COMMUNICATION GOALS

I will never forget the Sunday I was in church and our pastor mentioned several announcements during the beginning of the service. That day, I went home to grab lunch before driving to South Carolina. As I was making my sandwich, I attempted to remember what the announcements were that day. I couldn't remember any at that time because they only informed; they left no lasting impact. As I reviewed the bulletin, I saw the announcement. It read, "The altar guild needs more help. Don't you want to volunteer?" As I re-read the announcement, I remember the thought that went through my mind was something to the effect of, *Oh goodness, no!*

I remembered a bad experience from my younger days. It was an altar guild member who once told me that Jesus failed to show up for worship one Sunday because I had inadvertently lit the candle on the right prior to lighting the candle on the left! This is at least the way I now remember the story so many years later. So no, my immediate wish was not to join them.

Later, upon reflection, I remembered the story of my friend Stacy. She once told me that the month she serves on altar guild is the most spiritual month of her year. I was perplexed, but she shared that as she worked on Friday afternoon to set the table for Sunday, the sanctuary was empty and quiet. It was in this time that she felt her prayer life was the deepest as she prayed for her children, husband, and family. She went on to tell me that during that time setting the table, she reflected on her own journey of faith and the people who have led her to be the person she is today, and she prayed for them as well. She also shared that cleaning up after communion was not the chore she thought it was. Instead it was a joy to know that what she was cleaning up was the Lord's Supper, and that it was important to provide people a time to commune with our Lord.

After I remembered Stacy's story, I wondered why in the world our pastor would ask for volunteers. Why didn't he simply have Stacy tell her story? When I think about Stacy's story, even I might say, "Yes, I would like to serve on the altar guild because I too need a more spiritual month, and I would like time to focus my prayer life on those who I care about and love." Let's communicate outcome and inspiration so that more people will pay attention to what we communicate. If we communicate inspiration, more will join our work, and people will become even more excited to give.

Once again, let me make a distinction between goals and tactics. In the church we fail to differentiate between these two all the time. There is more on this in strategic planning, but the utilization of a website, bulletin, letter, Facebook page, and signage are communication tactics. The majority of our time should not be focused on the tactics. Our energy should be placed on our communication goals.

A sample communication goal could be, "Within eighteen months, 50 percent of our active families will be able to articulate at least one story of ministry impact that has taken place in the past year."

This goal is SMART.

Specific: active families (I will leave defining "active" to you)

Measurable: 50 percent of families

Achievable: this is quite possible to achieve

Relevant: the goal ties back to our mission

Time oriented: it will happen in eighteen months

In order to reach this goal, you likely need to use various tactics, including some video, live stories in worship, and written stories that get shared in a number of different places. If the goal is bold enough, you may have to engage the tactic of hiring someone to tell the stories. But don't assume that simply hiring someone will suddenly have the outcome you are looking for. If hiring a person is your goal, the impact will end there. Provide the new hire with SMART goals to work toward. Remember that most congregations will experience a tremendous growth in communication if they focus more on *what* they communicate and less time on *how*.

Another sample goal for communication could be, "Twenty families that have never worshiped here will attend worship at First Presbyterian Church on Christmas Eve this year." In order to achieve this goal, we need to define what needs families in our community may have and how those needs can be addressed by attending worship with us. A good place to start to determine the needs of those seeking a place for worship on Christmas Eve would be to talk to the families who visited last year. Then, create messages that align with those defined needs and get them placed in front of people who may have them so that they can engage the communication. This is more than simply announcing or even advertising your worship times. If we simply tell people that Christmas Eve worship is at 7:00 p.m. and 9:00 p.m., all we have told them is when we worship. We have told them nothing of why we worship on Christmas Eve and why they might want to join us. It is either arrogant or out-of-touch marketing—or both—to simply share worship times with nonchurch members and expect them to change behavior and join us. Doing this effectively is known as *needs-based marketing* or *benefit marketing*.

Once we know the goal, we can determine the tactics to achieve the goal. We know what the communication needs to be, and we determine where to place the communication tactics so that the right audience will be able to see it.

The goal should not be "to launch a Twitter account for the congregation." Launching a Twitter account could be a tremendous tactic to reach an audience that you aren't currently reaching, but you won't know that until you have a strong goal that you are working toward.

The only exception I will give to all of this is having a website. It is simply congregational malpractice to not have a functioning, up-to-date website in today's world. Your webpage is your church's front door today; it's the primary way people find you. If you don't make it easy for people to find your worship times, address, and contact information, people who are looking for you will likely look somewhere else.

Appendix A shares some outcome story samples and how to write them. As you are pulling together your generosity/stewardship team, a quality writer who enjoys discovering outcomes is likely one of the most important people to recruit. Finding someone who is creative at writing headlines is also quite important.

Quality, organized, and effective communication is critical in developing a culture of generosity in our congregations and leading to abundance. It takes intentionality to reach the point of communicating the proper messages effectively. Like a bee colony that is effectively communicating, a congregation that excels at communication will be positioned to thrive in today's world.

CHAPTER 7.

DONOR MENTALITY

The honeybee colony is fascinating because each bee is more focused on the colony than on its personal desires and goals. When a honeybee stings, it will die because the stinger rips apart its abdomen, and it no longer can sustain life. The decision to sting is made to benefit the colony over the life of the individual, and it is made without hesitation.

I sometimes long for donors to be like the honeybee, focused on the greater good and not on their own personalities, ideologies, and experiences. But alas, donors are individuals and must be treated as such. Too often, churches treat donors as if they have all reached the same place in their generosity journey and are all at the same spiritual maturity level. That is too simplistic. Donors are people, and people are not alike!

In chapter 2 of *Passing the Plate*, the authors lay out the following realities of giving by American Christians.

Fact #1: At least one out of five American Christians—20 percent of all U.S. Christians—gives literally *nothing* to church, parachurch, or nonreligious charities.

Fact #2: The vast majority of American Christians give *very* little to church, parachurch, or nonreligious charities.

Fact #3: American Christians do not give their dollars evenly among themselves but rather a small minority of generous givers among them contributes most of the total Christian dollars given.

Fact #4: Higher income–earning American Christians—like Americans generally—give less or no more as a percentage of household income than lower income–earning Christians.

Fact #5: Despite massive growth of real per-capita income in the twentieth century, the average percentage share of income given by American Christians not only did not grow in proportion but actually declined slightly during this same time period.

Fact #5: The vast majority of the money that American Christians do give to religion is spent in and for their own local communities of faith. Little is spent on missions, development, and poverty relief outside local congregations, particularly outside the United States, in ways that benefit people other than the givers themselves.[1]

These statistics and facts about giving can paint a very bleak picture for us. My hope, however, is that the challenging news drives us to focus on doing stewardship better. We need to get into the mind of the donor. Encounters are about more than asking donors for money. We need to spend time getting to know them, discovering how they interact with money, learning what ministry excites them, and discerning how to best approach them to help them grow. I also think the facts above reflect our inability to have a strategic vision and our ability to communicate our impact. This results in

1. Christian Smith, Michael O. Emerson, and Patricia Snell, *Passing the Plate: Why American Christians Don't Give Away More Money* (Oxford: Oxford University Press, 2008), 29–56.

less giving to our ministries than our donors have the capacity to provide.

In his book *Donors Are People Too*, Timothy Smith says we should spend no less than 80 percent of our time building trust with a donor.[2] In order for a donor to want to support your church, they must trust that you will do with their gift what you say you will do. This ties back to the case (see chap. 5). If all we will do with their gifts is balance a budget and not make an impact on the world, they will hold back.

I recently heard about a donor we had been working with in a church this year. The pastor and I noticed in May that donor #2 for their organization, a donor who typically provides $20,000 per year in support, was no longer making any financial gifts to the church. Instead of sending a "past due" notice, the pastor visited and listened. He discovered some hurt feelings. Yes, he mentioned that he noticed that they weren't giving, but he told them he was more interested in building trust, casting vision, and getting them excited about his leadership and where the church is heading. The pastor emailed me this week to let me know that $25,000 was coming this year at the end of the year, and a commitment for an additional $25,000 for next year was promised. The pastor shared this from the donor: "The key to this was to know your priorities for leading us and that you cared more about our hearts and minds than our money." The pastor developed trust and treated the donors like the people that they are. Honestly, he just did really good pastoral care.

Many of the larger donors to congregations are also

2. Timothy L. Smith, *Donors Are People Too: Managing Relationships with Your Ministry's Major Contributors* (Akron, OH: International Christian Publishing, 2003), 93.

making substantial gifts elsewhere. I once asked a million-dollar donor to an organization why he wasn't giving more to his congregation. His reply was, "My congregation can't handle more than I currently give them." In this case, the donor was right. All they talked about was balancing a budget and not giving raises to the staff. They lacked vision. They were bogged down in scarcity thinking. They lacked any sense of making a bigger impact in the world, and so he chose to make his larger gifts to places that had a better case for support and a stronger sense of impacting the world.

Donors want to make an impact in the world. They expect to hear about how that is happening with the gifts that they give to you. Yes, they want to know that you are responsible and will balance a budget. More importantly, they want to know that you have a vision, are working to implement that vision, and are learning on your journey to fulfilling that vision.

Donors want to partner with you. One of the highlights of my life was my time as a summer camp counselor. That experience taught me so much about myself and how to live in this world. My wife and I met on staff. I became a leader there. I discovered how to articulate my faith there. I'm now far too old to be a camp counselor anymore, but I want to continue to be part of that impactful ministry as it passes on faith and builds leaders for our church. So, we are donors to the camp. This is my way of a partnering with that ministry now. As a partner donor, I expect to hear stories of how campers are impacted with faith and of how counselors grow as leaders of our church by serving there. And I am not disappointed.

What do your donors want to help you accomplish? Are you telling them how their donations are having an impact? Henri Nouwen says it so well: "Indeed, if we raise funds for the creation of a community of love, we are helping build the kingdom. We are doing exactly what we are supposed to do as Christians."[3]

Ask yourself this one simple question: "If someone had an extra $100, why would they choose to give it to us rather than some other organization?" The answer to this question likely won't be the same for every donor to your church, but they will likely align. Donors give to vision and leaders. Cast a vision, and be a leader that takes the time to care for your donors. Establish trust with them, and they will choose your organization for the gift of their extra $100.

We sometimes hear about million-dollar gifts being given to organizations across the country, though most often these big gifts are not given to churches. Those million-dollar gifts are normally given to organizations with million-dollar visions. The same is true of $10,000 gifts and $10,000 visions. Donors are not going to give money to a church or other organization so that the organization can simply hold on to the money. Donors know that there is critical need out there in the world, and they want to be a part of addressing those needs. Get to know your donors to help align their passions with your ministry priorities.

Smith says, "The mission of your organization should be the foundation of every conversation you have with a major donor about your ministry."[4] Donors are interested in what your ministry is about and what it is doing. Let

3. Henri Nouwen, *A Spirituality of Fundraising* (Nashville: Upper Room, 2011), 25.

4. Smith, *Donors Are People Too*, 37.

them know the impact, share the stories of making a difference in the world, and they will respond generously.

Smith goes on to state, "It doesn't matter how old and established my ministry organization may be, if the donor feels I'm out of touch, his interests will gravitate elsewhere."[5] It takes regular communication with a donor to keep their interest and attention in your ministry. It isn't enough to publish a newsletter and assume a donor knows what we are doing and the impact we are having. It takes dialogue and getting to know our donors to understand their passions and priorities, and what they hope to accomplish with the resources God has provided them.

A donor I worked with when I was raising money for the camps once told me that they were shifting their focus to the seminary. I told them that I could appreciate that, but I asked them what it was about the seminary that excited them so much. They shared that their congregation had struggled to get a pastor, and they wanted to do what they could to ensure that leaders were being raised up for the church. I was able to share with them statistics and stories about how many former counselors from our camp were currently in seminary. I further shared a study about the impact outdoor ministry had on the call of pastors. I also shared my own call story and how camp was central to my call to ministry. The donor was overwhelmed by the place of the camps in accomplishing exactly what they were hopeful for. They not only continued to support the camps, but they expanded their support to care for the seminary. It wasn't an either/or for them, it was both/and. Had I not visited and known what they valued, the ministry would have lost a donor, and the

5. Smith, *Donors Are People Too*, 56.

donor would have missed a tremendous opportunity to achieve his or her goals.

When you take the time to get to know the mentality of your organization's donors, they won't feel like you just want their money. They will feel like you are a partner in advancing their values and making their money do for the world what they hope it will accomplish. Donors are people, and they deserve to be treated like the individuals that they are.

MOVING BEYOND CASH FLOW AND BALANCED BUDGET

In congregations, our ask sometimes assumes that every donor is motivated by a balanced budget or that their biggest concern is with the cash-flow issues of the congregation. We may send letters in September talking about how far behind we got in the summer and how short we are on cash. Or we send a letter in early December explaining how much money we need to balance the budget by the end of the year.

I have discovered that the people in a congregation who are most motivated by balanced budgets tend to be on the finance committee or serve on council. Their concern is understandable, since part of their work is to create and balance the budget. But be aware that many others in the congregation are not motivated in this way. Most donors want the organization to thrive and not just survive. Most donors want the congregation to make an impact and not just have enough cash to pay the bills. It is reasonable to tell people you need cash to operate, but if that is your primary message to donors, you need to know that you are not aligning with their priorities. You may get a little something from them, but you aren't going to receive gifts that reflect the passion of your donors.

I need to address one other type of donor mentality—the reluctant donor, or the person who has never been taught generosity. Not everyone grows up in a family that teaches or models generosity. When meeting with a group, I often ask the question, "Who taught you to be generous, and how did they teach you?" The answers tell me a lot. In a recent group session, I asked this question, and someone asked, "What if your parents didn't teach you to be generous?" I thanked her for her honesty and assured her she wasn't alone.

Many people think their money is their own, and nobody else should get access to it. I once had a person say to me, "Nobody is helping my kids with a camp scholarship, so why should I help someone else's kids?" These are tougher donors, but we cannot give up on them. We also need to recognize that it might take God a bit of time to work on their hearts. Be reminded that changing their heart is God's role. Our role is to remain positive about our ministry and continue to witness to a God who provides us a world of abundance.

The key to working with these tougher donors is to not let their attitude cause us to quit or to give us the false assumption that everyone is like them. I will talk more about them in the next chapter on roadblocks. As we learn about what motivates our donors, we begin to align our communication to encourage them further. We also need to let them communicate with one another by telling their stories. Donors need to learn that they aren't the only ones being generous in the congregation and need to learn from others how to be even more generous. Donors should never dictate your mission, but they should be invited into your mission to help you grow and expand it. As we take the time to listen to our donors, we will see how God is calling us to encourage others in their giving and to grow generosity across the church. Take the time to understand where our donors are in their journey and what motivates them to be generous. When you do this, you will be able to build a culture of generosity.

I will also say that you will be richly blessed. Donors have taught me more about generosity, passion, and desire to advance the kingdom of God than I can ever convey in this book. I am blessed to know these generous souls. They lift my faith and help me see God active and alive in this world. Many of our most generous donors are in fact like the bee that places the hive above self. They have passion for advancing the kingdom of God, and getting to know these generous people is a joy and privilege.

CHAPTER 8.

ROADBLOCKS

Anyone who keeps honeybees is aware of Varroa mites. These mites are devastating bee colonies more than anything else in the environment. Varroa mites suck the blood out of larvae and young bees and cause colonies to weaken and not survive the winter. During the spring and early summer, colonies tend to produce enough new bees that the mites don't overwhelm the colony. But when the queen starts laying fewer eggs for fall and winter, the mites continue to grow in population until the hive has too many mites per bee, which causes the bees to suffocate and die. This kills the colony in the winter and is responsible for most colony deaths in the United States today.

Just as mites cause the destruction of a bee colony, some members of our congregations can be roadblocks in our ministry that could ultimately lead to the death of our congregation. Based on decades of scarcity thinking as our model for ministry, we have developed plenty of "mites" that will suck the life out of our ministry if we aren't careful.

In many congregations, stewardship teams have either not been functioning or are not trained to do their work. When the stewardship team is not effective, the finance team begins to control the message regarding the budget, and the message is often one of scarcity. They reinforce that there is not enough money and often look to hold down spending or even make cuts. Generosity is not transactional. It's not like paying dues for a health club or paying for dinner when you go out to eat. Generosity happens when people recognize that what they have is a gift of God and seek to advance the kingdom of God through the sharing of their resources.

For the last several weeks, I have interacted with a finance team member who insists that we cut the budget because he doesn't believe that nonpledgers will continue the gift that they have given for each of the last several years. He bases his assumption on the fact that they didn't turn in a formal statement of intent. In my experience, unless people die, move, or get mad at the church, they are very likely to continue their pattern of giving. In this case, these nonpledgers have never pledged, but their giving pattern is very stable. There is no reason to cut revenue forecasts unless these people die, move, or have something significantly negative happen in their lives. We can watch their giving pattern and project their continued generosity.

In another church, a well-meaning council member said, "Let's ask people to each give $200 extra at the end of the year, and if everyone agrees to give this extra gift, we will have $3,000!" I quickly shot this down and left generosity open-ended for a myriad of potential ministries that would be implemented with extravagant generosity. Four donors gave more than $3,000 each themselves. Had we followed the idea that we live in a world of scarcity, we likely would have received a few gifts of $200. At the time of this writing, the congregation is up $15,000, which is much more than the scarcity-minded $200 each.

Additionally, we need to understand that $200 for each person is also not fair. For my family, a $200 gift can be made fairly easily, but I certainly remember when that was a stretch. We are not called to equal giving. We are called to equal sacrifice. Let me give $2,000, while others give $200; others give $20,000, and still others give $20. All are significant gifts given according to our means.

Sometimes, the mites in our congregation will say, "We can't do that; our congregation is giving all they can." This is true for a limited vision. However, when we tie our vision to impact, it will surprise even the most blood-sucking mite that God can do even more. You see, we should never say no for anyone. And, we should not assume that everyone else in the congregation is in the same situation as we are. The disciples tried to say no on behalf of the people when Jesus fed the five thousand. Instead of saying no on behalf of the people, Jesus rejected scarcity and asked each to share what they had available.

The hardest lesson I learned as vice president for the camps was that not everyone gave as I was inclined to give. Many lived in their world of stuff and didn't give money away, but others demonstrated generosity that even I could not imagine. Those who shared so willingly reminded me of Jesus's story of the widow who gave a mite, all she had, as an offering. The gift was small but extravagantly generous (Mark 12:41–44).

PLACING LIMITS

One practice that I have seen limit a congregation's giving is when the leadership offers the congregation what I call a "list of stuff" to give money to. The items on the list might not be inspiring and don't seem to align with the mission and vision. I recently read what is supposed to be a case statement from a congregation. This is what I heard as I read through it.

- We need to help our youth by replacing ceiling tiles in the youth room.

- We need more volunteers to help our education take place.

- Our last pastor had free health care as a member of the military, and now we will have to pay the nearly $20,000 for healthcare for the new pastor.

All of the above may be true, but none of it is helpful in spurring generosity. The ceiling tiles may be in terrible shape, but nobody will feel they are helping the youth by replacing ceiling tiles. By mentioning a lack of volunteers, I am left feeling like the congregation can't implement anything. And by not preparing for paying for health insurance in the past, it makes me feel like we can't manage for the future.

I have also seen congregations prepare a list of twelve things that they are going to launch when money is given for them. The list of items often seems to have little or nothing in common with anything else on the list. It just looks like we simply asked every committee what they want to do and said they could have it all (if the dollars come in to support). We need goals to tie the list together. We need the goals to support the mission. It all works together. Do you see how these first three steps (board leadership, the stewardship plan, and strategic vision) keep relating back to each other?

This year, I had a congregation call me to say, "We have been living off of our reserves for the last five years, and we are going to run out in two years." They had heard that congregations that work with us often grow their annual fund 15 percent in the first year and wondered if we could work together. We started that work, and we shared with the congregation that I would be guiding them. Immediately, a well-meaning former financial secretary sent a letter to the council stating that he knew the giving of the congregation and that all the generous families had died. The secretary suggested they should just start cutting spending since the current congregation was giving all they could.

Well, in the next call with the stewardship team, I mentioned my desire for them to secure a $5,000 challenge gift to stimulate a statement of intent from more families than ever, and immediately someone on the team offered the gift. Apparently, not every family was giving all that they could. We simply sent a response back to this person who thought the congregation was giving all they could that we appreciated their passion for the congregation but that our experience with the potential generosity was very different. We grew giving in this congregation in South Carolina by $45,060, or 23 percent, this year, with 90 percent of respondents increasing their giving. It is good we didn't listen to the roadblock.

The finance team has a very important job in the church. Good accounting and financial forecasting are critical to decision making. What is not helpful is when that finance committee mistakes its role for one of control. The finance team should tell us how much money has been given and how much is spent. But leadership should make decisions on where we will invest for the future and what risks we will take to see new ministry happen and to see growth take place.

In another congregation the treasurer told the council that they couldn't spend money on a new campaign that was going to expand capacity and was designed to lead to growth. She was adamant. The treasurer felt the money they were going to spend needed to remain in reserves to cover scarcity in the lean months. This treasurer over-stepped. It is her job to point out options, not to get in the way. If leadership believes in their vision and mission and believes that growth will happen as result of their plans, they need to take risks. I'm not advocating for misman-agement and free-spending, but total risk aversion will lead to decline and ultimately to the death of organiza-tions.

I personally think God will be grateful if we, as the church, take a few more risks. I think God will be happier if we take risks and fail than if we remain so passive that we just die a slow, painful death.

My preference for church leadership is that the finance committee reports on where we are with expenses, while the stewardship team takes responsibility for the projec-tion of revenue. The finance team will often say we can't do something because we don't have the money for it. I want the stewardship team to stand up and say, "No wor-ries, we will raise a bit more to make this critical ministry happen."

NEVER SAY NO

We also need to learn to never say no on behalf of anyone. Have you ever had someone in the congregation say, "We just increased giving for our annual fund, so we couldn't possibly ask anyone for anything else this year"? As long as we are not asking for money just for the sake of more money, we don't need to worry about this. If we have ministry opportunities that will help us live out our mission and accomplish our vision, we need to give people opportunities to make that happen. When giving makes an impact, it is an opportunity. We don't need to apologize for asking to address the need. People want the money they have to make a difference, and we owe it to our people to provide places for them to give gifts to make a difference in the world for God's work.

When faced with roadblocks, we owe it to our ministry to work through those challenges. Our ministry is important, even critical, and we cannot allow a roadblock to cause it to stop. In some situations, we need to work on a solution to the roadblock that allows at least some growth to happen, even if it isn't on the timetable that we would want. In other cases, we need to lead right through the roadblock and boldly bring about the future. Making the transition from scarcity to abundance happens when we work through these roadblocks and cast a vision for a future where ministry is thriving.

We cannot be held captive by one or two voices who are holding the ministry back. This can be a challenge as these people are also often our friends. But the gospel needs to be proclaimed. Those who are hurting need care. The hungry need to be fed. Everyone needs to worship. If we believe our mission to be critical, we will work tirelessly through the challenges that arise, even when that might make us a little uncomfortable.

NEGATIVE VOICES AND CHALLENGING QUESTIONS

In just about every campaign I have led, at least one negative voice will arise, questioning what we are about or the tactics we are employing to move the ministry forward. When this happens, I feel like we are likely pushing hard enough. I don't ever want anyone to be offended by the work we do. But growth doesn't tend to happen unless we get challenged or take the time to look at things differently.

In his address to the Association of Lutheran Development Executives, I heard Jerold Panas share that 73 percent of donors voice three objections to a proposal. They don't object because they are against what you are asking for. More often they are determining whether or not you are serious about what you are raising money for and if it is worth their investment. When we back down from their objections, these donors think we didn't know what we are doing or don't really believe in the project. Donors are just trying to make certain that their money will be invested to impact the world for the kingdom of God.

Pastors need to be reminded that questions are not necessarily bad. In fact, I look at questions as opportunities. Questions mean that someone is paying enough attention to find out more. In a campaign for a new facility, one couple must have asked thirty questions. The campaign chair asked me if we could move on. I shared that we would answer questions as long as people had them. This particular congregation once had a campaign that did not result in the facility being completed, and donors felt cheated. Well, this couple asked all their questions, and two days later they presented the pastor with a check for $500,000. They were checking whether it was worth their investment.

I'm not sure why people in church leadership are so averse to having questions asked. Most people don't ask questions out of hostility. They ask questions out of a desire to be brought more intimately into the ministry that is taking place. We should embrace the opportunity to help grow a donor's heart to be more closely aligned with the work that we are doing. Questions are not a threat. They are an invitation. Embrace the dialogue.

As a beekeeper, I could give up on the hobby because the mites devastate the hive and make it far harder to keep bees alive today. However, I keep working at it. I keep experimenting and trying new things. And I am rewarded with that perseverance as I am now getting more hives through the winter, and they become more capable of producing more honey. The mites are a roadblock to bee-keeping. At the same time, they have helped me learn more and become better. The roadblocks in our congregation can make us better as a church. They will push us to articulate our message, tell our story, focus on our mission, and advance our ministry. The result will be congregations better living into what God is calling us to be. Sometimes we need to figure out how to work with the roadblocks, and other times we need to drive right through them. The key is to not allow the roadblocks to win and keep you from the goal, because the goal is a stronger church that has much more vitality and makes a difference in people's lives. The goal is to live in the abundance that we believe God provides.

CHAPTER 9.

UTILIZE VOLUNTEERS

Honeybees are independent creatures. However, without the intervention of the volunteer beekeeper, honeybee colonies will die today. It takes a beekeeper to help break the mite cycle either by removing the queen for a period of time or by introducing a chemical treatment to kill the mites. Without the volunteer beekeeper, the colony will not thrive.

The most effective nonprofits in the United States utilize volunteers to reach new donors and help donors reach a new level of generosity. The same is true in the church. In my time working for the camps, the largest gift I received was given by the best friend of one of our board members. The volunteer board member made the introduction, and the donor was delighted to make the gift, which was made in honor of his friend.

In the church, peers asking peers is most effective. How many times have you heard someone say, "Well, I'm on a fixed income, and can only give so much"? It is difficult for the paid staff person to respond to this statement. But in the same situation, a volunteer could respond by providing their personal example and saying, "Well, my income is fixed too, but I have other financial resources that I can share and still not be in danger of outliving my retirement." The excuse doesn't get to become the story. Or the volunteer can share how they sacrifice something of importance as an example of how generosity can grow.

When a volunteer says, "Join me in making a gift," it gives other donors permission to be generous in a way they had not imagined. Or when a volunteer says, "I learned that at my age a great way for me to give is directly from my IRA," a donor will hear the message very differently than when a paid staff person who is much younger tells them about that type of giving.

Volunteers help authenticate fundraising efforts by their involvement. I often say that no one wants to be the only generous donor to a campaign. If there is solid volunteer support, and all volunteers give before asking the rest of the constituency, we guarantee that someone will not be the only generous donor to a campaign because the volunteers are already on board and their generosity can be shared.

Furthermore, the best ask is the one that happens face to face. Congregational staff, especially at a church, are not large enough to ask everyone face to face while still doing their other jobs. By gathering volunteers to help with the asking, or at least asking for the response, response rates will go way up.

When staff control every aspect of the fundraising activity, it can feel very organization driven, which is not helpful to the outcomes of the appeal. Staff-driven appeals often miss in the messaging; paid staff sometimes do not fully understand what motivates donors.

ENGAGING VOLUNTEERS IN STEWARDSHIP

Here are some of my favorite methods of engaging volunteers in congregational stewardship.

- **Case development**: The case should be written and articulated by volunteers so that the congregation feels ownership of it.

- **Temple talks** (also called *mission moments* or *testimonies*): These are used to help inspire the congregation to give to the ministry outcomes of the congregation.

- **Generosity story writers**: Help members discern the story of how they learned to be generous so they can share their stories with the congregation and help mentor others.

- **Leadership gifts**: Having the volunteers and council give their gifts before the rest of the congregation helps set the pace and demonstrate generosity for the remainder in the congregation.

- **Every member visit**: By far the most effective response strategy is to have members visit in the homes of their peers to ask them to participate in the appeal and to share their own support of the appeal.

- **Phonathon follow-up**: Having volunteers call those who have not provided a response tends to ensure a good final result in number of intent cards collected. Much work needs to be done in congregations to obtain cell numbers if this effort is to realize its full potential.

- **Offering moments**: I like to have someone offer a very short (forty-five second) teaching about stewardship during the time of the offering to help teach the congregation why we give.

LARGER CONGREGATIONS

It seems that the larger the congregation, the harder it is to give responsibility for stewardship over to volunteers. The reality is that the effective engagement of volunteers in the annual fund will lead to significantly larger and more substantial giving. It will also lead to a necessary culture shift around generosity and abundance. Some ideas for larger congregations to consider are as follows.

- **Cottage gathering hosts**: The more intimate we can be with our donors, the greater the growth that will take place. Recruit a group of people who will host a home gathering for ten to twenty families at which they will be informed about the goals of the stewardship drive and motivated to participate. It is also helpful for the hosts to present the ask and follow up with this group until their intent cards are in. I would also task these hosts with gathering further information about those who are invited to their gathering. Find out what excites the donors most. Find out what their passions are so that when a new goal is introduced, they can be invited to participate more deeply according to their passions.

- **Case testing**: In larger congregations, it is critical that staff members test the case for gifts with people not on staff so that they can determine how well it resonates with the congregational members.

- **Lead donor selection and rating**: Staff often do not know the capacity of donors the way that fellow congregational members can understand this. Income disparity among the nonprofit and for-profit sectors is significant, therefore peer review is critical in determining ask amounts.

- **Generosity small-group leadership**: Many larger congregations have a small-group network. Volunteers can get to each of these groups to lead a session on generosity to help people mentor one another in how they learned generosity.

- **Inspiration testing**: Sharing inspiration is among the hardest activities in our congregations today because we are accustomed to focusing on sharing information. Encourage a group of volunteers to test and reflect on how we are inspiring, and determine additional methods for us to improve how we are doing this. In one congregation I work with, the pastor has a group of three people who meet monthly so the pastor can practice telling the outcome stories of the congregation. This group helps her discern which stories are most effective and what part of the stories resonate best with the membership.

Engaging volunteers is critical for expanding your mission and for aligning the members closer to the work of the church. However, it is critical as you engage your donors in volunteer activity that they find the work meaningful, a good use of their time, and faith enriching.

If volunteer service feels trite or is viewed as a waste of time, they will think their financial giving to the church is also just a waste of money. And it will stifle their interest in growing generosity to new levels. However, if they feel the service they are giving has a tremendous impact, they will feel their financial gifts are also critical for expanding that impact.

RECRUITING VOLUNTEERS

I hear pastors and congregational members alike saying it is harder to recruit volunteers today. That may be a true statement. This reality means that we have to change our recruitment tactics. Having people fill out a "Time/ Talent" form, which lists activities they aren't sure make a difference in the world, can be wasted effort. People will no longer self-select to make themselves busier. They want their time to make an impact. They will gladly invest their time if you can articulate why their participation matters. Do what you can to discover the needs people have and how their service will activate those needs. When the investment of time aligns with need or passion, they will find fulfillment.

A pastor once told me that nobody would serve on his finance team. I asked him, "How fulfilling is it to serve on the finance team?" He said it really isn't and, in fact, that it was probably the worst job in the church. I told him that I wouldn't serve on the finance team either. Before recruiting finance team members, I suggested he needed to find ways to make it more fulfilling. We need to eliminate unfulfilling work from the church. Some activities can be eliminated, and we will be just fine. Others can be outsourced so that we don't burn out our people if there is no meaning in the service.

I'm not sure that announcing in a bulletin that you need volunteers for a project and then not having anyone reply to it would actually indicate that people are not interested in helping. It might just mean that recruiting through bulletin announcements is ineffective. I often ask people, "How many disciples did Jesus recruit with a bulletin announcement?" Of course, the question is asked with tongue in cheek. But the point is, Jesus recruited by inviting disciples on a face-to-face, personal level.

Just as the formula for asking for gifts is Inform-Evaluate-Inspire-Ask-Thank, the same is true in recruiting volunteers. In fact, I suggest you spend as much or more time motivating them for the roles you need them to take than you do informing them about what the work entails.

For example, I once became an usher, not because I wanted to be one, but because someone asked my son if he would like to do it and if I would like to join him in that role. It was very effective, but it was because I was asked that I chose to participate. I didn't respond to a bulletin announcement. I responded to a real person inviting me. Serving with my son was also very motivating for me.

TACTICS FOR GREATER VOLUNTEER RECRUITMENT

I hear people say today that it's always the same people who do a greater share of the work and that it is hard to get new people involved. Let's not blame the people not involved. Let's take a look at our recruiting tactics. I have found the following tactics to be effective in growing the number of volunteers in our congregations.

- **Create a job description.** Offer people insight into exactly what you are looking for in the position. This is informing.

- **Tell people why you think they would be good at the job.** Let people know that you have been praying about their involvement. Let them know why their gifts are perfectly suited, or even better, tell them what you think they will get out of the service to grow in their faith.

- **Let people know who else they will be working with.** An important part of the engagement is knowing who they get to interact with and have mentor them.

- **Promise them training and resources.** Don't recruit volunteers and have them figure things out.

- **Have term or time limits.** I prefer to have an option where the obligation needs to be renewed by both the volunteer and the church. It's not reasonable to expect people to take positions of power for life, and we don't want people feeling they are required to serve a life sentence on a team.

- **Check in with your volunteers.** Engage them not just to ask what they need and how it is going, but also to discover how they see God at work through their service. I think one of the greatest gifts a pastor can give a volunteer is the gift of discerning where God is at work through their service. The volunteer might get bogged down in the task and forget to look for God's activity through their work. Be present to help them figure out what God is up to.

I know someone who volunteers through his congregation to feed meals to veterans. He loves this work and is part of it every time his congregation has the responsibility. He likes to serve, but if you ask him, he will tell you the real reason is that he remembers his dad every time that he serves meals to veterans. He and his father were not very close, but his dad was a veteran. As he interacts with and meets the veterans, he is reminded of the love he had for his father. Most people would look at the veteran meal service as something that the church needed people to do. This person reminds us that service is something that we need to do in order to be more complete. Our messaging for volunteers rightly focuses on what we need them to do for the church. But we also need to remind them what God will do through them and to them because of their service.

In the honeybee hive, there are no retired bees. Each bee has a fulfilling job that leads to vibrancy in the hive. We need the same in our churches. We need people engaging in service. We need people who are adding to the mission and vision of the congregation and helping us to fulfill our goals, objectives, and tactics to usher in the kingdom of God. At the same time, the congregation owes it to our volunteers to provide meaningful service that leads to spiritual and personal growth.

CHAPTER 10.

DONOR STEWARDSHIP

The life cycle of a honey bee is egg, pupa, larva, house bee, and field bee, and then the bee dies. They only get to go through the cycle one time. For the colony to survive, more eggs must be laid so that the process can start over again.

Fortunately, the life cycle of a donor is not "one and done." It can be repeated, and we don't have to find new donors all the time. Managing donor stewardship is critical for churches and nonprofit organizations. It is common in many churches for donors to stagnate at a certain giving level. Congregation leaders often believe the myth that their people are giving all they can. Congregations even do things such as keeping the budget flat to show donors that they don't need to grow their giving. However, by recognizing where donors are and then stewarding them over time, donors can grow to the point of making a major gift according to their means.

Our firm uses the following pyramid to demonstrate where donors can grow with your church. Only once in my career have I heard of a donor making an estate gift to an organization without any annual fund history. Most often, donors start at the bottom of the pyramid and work their way up to the top. It is our job to steward them through that journey. I call it a generosity journey.

The Pyramid of Giving

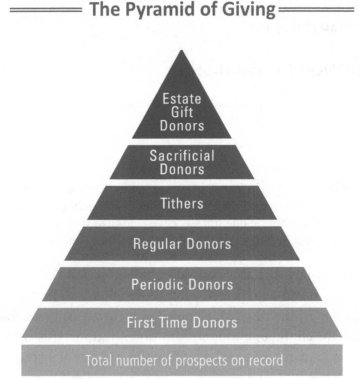

Estate
Gift
Donors

Sacrificial
Donors

Tithers

Regular Donors

Periodic Donors

First Time Donors

Total number of prospects on record

The pyramid shape is used to illustrate that the larger the gift sought, the fewer the prospects for such gifts. And, the fewer the prospects, the fewer the number of gifts.

I've heard church leaders say that it takes seven donors to replace one key donor who has learned and lived out generosity. That may be true if you aren't constantly working to help people grow in their generosity, but if you are helping your periodic donors move to being regular donors and your regular donors to tithers, then it isn't so devastating to lose one of your sacrificial donors.

As you see how the pyramid works, I hope you will understand that because people are at different places on the pyramid, it is okay to not treat everyone the same. The approach to a periodic donor is very different than the approach to a sacrificial donor. We shouldn't necessarily try to move a first-time donor to an estate donor, and certainly don't be disappointed that they don't move to this highest level of giving in one step. We communicate with and treat people differently depending on where they are on the pyramid.

UNDERSTANDING THE PYRAMID

Here is a deeper look at each category of donor on the pyramid of giving.

- **Total number of prospects on record**: This includes everyone in your database that has not made a financial gift. Many of these are confirmed youth or college students. In this section, I would pay the most attention to those who you deem capable of a gift. However, you need to know that from a financial perspective, this group takes the most energy and time to grow in their giving and often does not grow even with our best efforts. From a spiritual perspective, you should spend a little time here, but invest more energy into stewarding other donors. Again, moving this group to becoming an active donor is the hardest and most time-consuming work in growing generosity. I believe we owe it to this group to help them become generous, but spending too much time here will come at the cost of growing people who are more likely to support you with significant generosity. Growth with this group is much more likely for project giving than for a regular gift to the annual ministry budget.

- **First-time donors**: Effective nonprofits will have a special process they follow when someone contributes a first-time gift. Don't make the mistake of ignoring them and sending a statement to them at the end of the year. Congregations need to develop a process for tracking and following up with first-time donors. By making a gift to your congregation, donors are stating they are interested. How the congregation responds will determine how interested they remain. These donors provide a great opportunity for you to demonstrate how interested you are in them. Most nonprofits send thank-yous to donors within forty-eight hours. We should strive to do the same.

- **Periodic donors**: Most of the smallest donors to a congregation fall into this category. This category deserves attention over the long term, but it will not result in an immediate, large increase in generosity. As a consultant, I really enjoy working with congregations over the long term to develop donors in this category and the next category to build a longer-term, more sustainable funding pattern for the congregation. This strategy means the few donors at the top of your giving period are no longer overly burdened with the survival of the ministry. Growing these periodic donors takes intentionality over the long term. These donors have a need for mentors to teach them about a God of abundance, and they have a need to learn more about the impact that their giving over time can have in order to move up to the next level.

In a recent annual stewardship effort, one congregation grew two donors each by more than 2,000 percent. Each of those came from this category.

- **Regular donors**: These donors normally give monthly or at least give when they are in worship on a regular basis. It is at this level that generosity begins to really grow as regular gifts over time add up to significant amounts. A gift of $1 per day will likely be growth for most periodic donors and move them into this category, and if they will grow by that in a single year, I am usually pretty satisfied. Again, growing this group year after year will assure the stable financial footing for a congregation so that the loss of a sacrificial donor is not devastating to the organization. This group often responds to challenge gifts, and the generosity of others will stimulate them to grow in their giving.

- **Generous donors**: Since I don't like to use the words *tithe* or *tithers* or get caught up in the legalistic 10 percent, I prefer to include in this category those who are seeking to give a specific amount or percentage each year as a statement of their faith. They certainly provide gifts that are significant according to their means. These donors have a great grasp of generosity, and they give in order to make a difference in the world. They should never be taken for granted. People in this category will often have capacity to grow further if the case is aligned with their passions.

- **Sacrificial donors**—This group normally makes up 10 percent or less of a congregation's donors and gives significant amounts of their annual income to the church. This group is likely giving between 50 and 70 percent of a congregation's annual revenues. They are passionate about the ministry of the church. Many of them can still grow in their giving and are most happy to do so if others will join them. They don't want to be solely relied on to sustain the ministry, as they know the dangers of that. They also know that their giving is critical to the congregation. If invited to become partners in stimulating generosity from others, they will be happy to become inspirational participants through challenge and matching gifts. They should never be treated as ATMs that will bail out the congregation in a bind. When they are treated that way, they will resent the congregation, and you will unintentionally stifle giving from everyone else.

- **Estate gift donors**: The ultimate gift anyone can give an organization is a portion of their estate. I have known donors who leave enough behind to maintain their annual fund giving forever. Others leave an estate gift to accomplish a ministry into perpetuity. Still others tithe their estate or adopt the congregation as an additional child for estate-planning purposes. Congregations need to have gift-acceptance policies and a plan for these gifts. Members also need to be asked for them. Normally estate gifts are utilized for something permanent like facility growth or an endowment. This is the topic for another book, but ultimately it is healthy to have at least 10 percent and preferably 20 percent of the annual ministry revenue provided by endowment earnings. The key is to leverage those earnings and not allow them to stifle giving from others. Estate donors should be thanked during their lifetime, so processes to identify who has included the ministry in their estate is a critical task. Establishing a heritage society is an effective tactic in encouraging estate gifts.

APPROACHING DONORS

With each of these categories of donors we need to be sure that we inform, evaluate, inspire, ask, thank, and repeat.

INFORM

Let me repeat that simply sharing information is not enough to inspire, sustain, and grow donors. For example, when we communicate that we are far behind on our budget, what message do we send to a first-time visitor or a donor who just doubled their giving? Or if we mention for fifty-two weeks in a row that the youth group needs more money for a trip, the only message we are sharing is that there isn't enough. Sometimes our information reinforces a scarcity mentality, and I believe this is truly by accident.

Bulletins are great places to share information about what a youth group hopes to accomplish on a mission trip. Or a committee can share an outcome of what their effort yielded toward a goal. Bulletins can be a great place to share with people the purpose of our Wednesday evening Lenten services rather than just the times of those services. But we need to take great care that the information we share is the information needed to help someone to make the decision that we want them to make. Much of the information shared in congregations is misplaced and misaligned for the outcome we seek. It is helpful to audit the information shared and reflect on the question, "Does the information shared enable the target audience to make the decision that I desire that they make?"

EVALUATE

Evaluating donors in the congregation setting can be an intimidating process to consider. I often hear, "They are my friends, I worship with them, and I have never thought about how much they might be able to contribute." In some ways, I appreciate this sentiment. We should accept everyone in our congregation for who they are. However, it is through evaluation that we can help someone who is a moderate donor grow to a large donor or a small donor to a moderate donor.

My business partner, Dave Brunkow, tells the story of a congregation that needed to expand staff to call an associate pastor. The stewardship team spent significant time discerning who they thought could consider significant increases to their giving to ensure the new pastor's salary was covered and that they could call this person to serve in their parish with the confidence that they could cover the salary. They fully covered the salary only because they chose to evaluate who could consider making significant growth in their giving. The people responded generously because they had passion for the project and the ability to make the gift.

In the congregational setting, I rarely if ever encourage using any type of wealth screen on members. A wealth screen is a tool used to find out the net worth of a person and is commonplace among colleges, hospitals, and other large nonprofits. It is the job of leadership to get to know your people. Get to know who they are and what their passions are. Get to know what type of resources they might have that can be deployed for your ministry vision. Discover what projects align with what excites them and whether they have the resources to make a project happen.

INSPIRE

When I started working for the camps in North Carolina, they had a culture of sharing outcome stories of the ministry. I understand it took some time, but once the culture took hold, it was incredibly fulfilling to hear of all the ways God was impacting the world through the campers, counselors, and other leaders. Most of the churches I work with struggle significantly with motivation. Most of the time in the first year of consulting, we can move them to sharing appropriate and even exciting information, but motivation often seems to have fallen out of the DNA of the church. Too often we focus on being busy rather than outcome. I find that very few people care about busyness. They care a tremendous amount about effectiveness. Motivation focuses on the outcome and effectiveness of the ministry. Motivation is most often experienced as people share intimate, personal stories. This require a vulnerability that we are often not accustomed to in the church setting.

When we think about motivation, we think about what difference our ministry has on the lives of people. We focus less on offering too many activities and instead focus on ministry that makes a difference. We will have fewer pastors burn out if we focus more on impact and less on activity, because impact is the reason that most of our pastors followed the call into ordained ministry. They did not become pastors to fill their days with busywork. They want to see and experience God active in the world. Let's take time to look for how God is active through the work we do, remind ourselves of that, and share it with our donors. Outcome stories need to be communicated both in staff meetings and more widely so that all of our members hear them and can articulate how God is impacting the world through our ministry.

ASK

Asking is what scares most people away from serving on a stewardship team. Not everyone is equipped by God to be a good asker. Still, asking people directly is critical, and people like to be asked. I just completed a training for pastors on asking for major gifts. I started with an exercise in which participants first took time to get to know someone else attending the workshop. They each presented their case for their gifts and then asked for it. The first comment from one of the attendees was how nice it felt to be asked.

Our first instinct is to think that by asking people we may offend them. I suppose it is possible to offend someone by asking, but I have found offending by asking is a very difficult thing to do. I truly believe that more people are offended by not being asked. By not talking about giving, some people may harbor feelings of shame about their giving.

I've stated before that most congregations report how

much money they need to cover the budget in the coming year, and this is the basis of the stewardship drive. Or sometimes they focus on how much was given last year and tell people that decisions about what ministry to implement will be made after their donors indicate how much they will give. This is not effective asking.

We can also inadvertently put too much responsibility on individuals to decide what to give when we put a dollar number target in front of them, such as $400,000, $700,000, or even over $1 million, which is the total budget goal. Revealing budgetary spending targets certainly must be done, but if we focus solely on the big number, we can cause our smaller donors to think that their gifts don't matter or feel shame that they don't have enough to make a difference.

After I led a workshop in Virginia Beach, a woman approached me who was very emotional from the presentation. You see, I had told the people that if any of them currently gave less than $300 per year that, on behalf of their congregation, I was asking them to consider a gift of $1 per day in the coming year. She shared with me that she was one of those people. She also shared that she skipped worship in October in order to avoid the shame of hearing the stewardship drive. Additionally, she told me she would not serve on congregation council because she knew she was not a leader in giving. However, she could do $1 per day, and that would be a 40 percent increase for her giving. She also shared that she thought she could do more than this. By being asked, she finally felt like she could do her part to address the overall need. By not being asked, she was left to feel like she didn't have enough, and her gift was not important. Even larger donors like to know what they need to do as their part of the overall need. It is by asking people to grow in an appropriate way that people will get traction on their generosity journey.

By the way, saying "Whatever you can give would be great" is not asking. It is also not great! It is important in asking that we invite people to "consider" an amount. It can be a single amount or a range taken from the gift chart, but it needs to be specific, and it needs to be tailored to them. And asking should always invite people to greater generosity.

THANK

Finally, we need to thank people for their generosity. In today's world, thanking people has two elements: gratitude and accountability. The church needs to show gratitude for the resources that people choose to share with it. People have options for where to invest, so we need to thank them for choosing our congregation. Then we need to be accountable to donors by letting them know what we are accomplishing with their gifts and how those gifts are helping us accomplish the mission and goals we have said we will accomplish. As I have mentioned, I grew up with Jim and Tammy Faye Bakker misusing money. Television evangelists and others continue to do this today. We need to demonstrate accountability, and we need to let people know we are using their gifts as intended and that those gifts make an impact.

All five steps—Inform, Evaluate, Motivate, Ask, and Thank—are each critically important. If we move directly from informing to asking, the donor is left thinking the congregation just wants their money. Failure to inspire will leave your donors feeling that they are just there to give you money for stuff. Have you ever heard someone say "We have donor fatigue"? If you have, you are familiar with an organization that has failed to inspire their donors before asking. There is no such thing as donor fatigue when people are inspired. You may find an instance where a donor says, "I need to sit out this solicitation," but as long as you are inspiring them regarding the work you are about, they will be excited to stick with the congregation and continue as your partner in ministry.

Remember, every communication is a donor communication if a donor engages it. Let's make certain that our communications are engaging this cycle to help our donors make the best gifts they can. My prayer for what this section has demonstrated is that generosity to the church isn't just an issue of wealth. Donor generosity to the church is dependent on a careful process of aligning the impact of the ministry with the passions of the donor and engaging the donor in a process to grow more deeply in partnership with the ministry.

The good news here is that donors are not like bees. You do get a longer life cycle. You can ask again and continually invite them to grow. I have found that donors appreciate becoming more deeply engaged in the ministry as they progress through the donor pyramid and through the cycle of being cultivated, asked, and thanked for their gift.

With people in so many different places in their generosity journey, this can seem like a daunting task. However, remember that working toward a culture of abundance in the congregation can take time. You don't have to focus on each group every year. However, as the culture begins to change, donors will begin to cultivate each other. Volunteers will expand your reach, and your communication will be more effective and reach more people in their unique journeys in growing in generosity.

PART III.

STIMULATING GENEROSITY AND REINFORCING ABUNDANCE

This section is less theoretical and more practical. It is important to remember that this book addresses the first three key steps of our Ten Steps, so this is by no means meant to be an exhaustive playbook for the congregation.

CHAPTER 11.

COUNCIL AND BOARD ACTIVITIES

This past summer, I had what is known as a "hot hive." Basically, the queen was constantly releasing a pheromone that told the bees they were under attack. When I opened the lid, they were all over me in an incredibly aggressive manner. The only way to fix this situation is to find the queen, kill her, and then introduce a new queen. Almost immediately after this is done, the hive will calm down and return to normal. This is the worst part of beekeeping as you have thousands of bees trying not just to sting you, but kill you. However, once you get the hive re-queened, it becomes a very strong hive that produces quite a bit of honey and becomes docile.

Councils and boards need to focus on doing the right activities to lead organizations in the right directions. By introducing the best methods for meetings and work, we move organizations in the right direction. Board and council members that produce the wrong "pheromone" will lead the organization to act in ways that are dangerous to its future and to those who interact with it.

Serving on a congregation council or governing board should be the highlight of someone's service to the congregation and the culmination of their leadership journey. However, it is true that nominating committees often struggle to find people willing to serve. In some places, I don't blame people for not wanting to serve. In my first call, our council meetings often lasted over three and sometimes four hours. We spent more time on the minutiae than on the big picture and future activities. We would do a planning retreat weekend after the budget was already passed to decide what we would do in the next year. And we had people who obviously had a bad day at work come and take it out on us. I know congregations today who are struggling to find anyone to be president.

I once attended a synod council meeting and was intrigued to witness that the bishop did all the talking and spent a lot of time reading his report. In addition, the decisions made by the council were pretty mundane and straightforward. The meeting lasted five hours. After the meeting, I asked several questions about why things were the way they were, and the response was that this is how the predecessors did it. Fortunately, there was good leadership there, and it transformed over time.

PURPOSEFUL MEETINGS

Just because things used to be done in a certain way doesn't mean you still have to do them that way. Make sure the time is well spent. Every meeting should have not only an agenda but also a purpose. If we don't have a purpose for a meeting, we should cancel or postpone it until we have one. We should not waste people's time. It won't be meaningful if we don't have a purpose.

CREATE AN AGENDA

I once believed that part of the problem with the congregation council was that it had too many meetings. Most boards can do their work with quarterly meetings or even less. Meetings too often result in dealing with issues for management and not governance. However, one pastor shared with me the need to meet monthly in order to mentor and grow the council members into the leaders he needed. His meetings had the purpose of coaching the council members into greater leadership capacity and spiritual depth, and the members of the council were incredibly committed to the work of the church because of this.

If we want people to reflect positively on their time in leadership, we should be sure to respect their time. Have a time allocation for each meeting, and stick to it. Don't get bogged down in mundane discussions. Utilize en bloc actions in order to handle routine business. Have people agree to show up prepared and do things that make a difference. This work should be highly focused on the strategic plan and either its creation or its implementation. If it isn't in the strategic plan, it shouldn't be getting much of your energy at council meetings. If we do this, regardless of the frequency of the meetings, people will find their period of leadership fulfilling and worth the time they devote to this service.

COUNCIL JOB DESCRIPTIONS

In addition to having an agenda for the meeting, have job descriptions for membership on council and then honor those descriptions. Don't ask more of people than the description calls for, but honor the high calling that council leadership has by spelling it out on paper so people know what they are committing to through their service.

OPENING WITH DEVOTIONAL REFLECTIONS

Put energy into devotions for the council. Starting council meetings with devotional reflections can set the tone for the meeting. I assure you nobody will feel inspired by unplanned devotionals, so take time to prepare. For example, think about the agenda and the big-picture vision that has been or is being developed by leadership. Imagine how Scripture reading or prayers or other devotional reflections connect with the work the council will be addressing.

FOCUS ON OUTCOME STORIES

My favorite activity to do with council members is to share outcomes stories and teach them how to share those stories with others. My favorite opening to a council meeting is to have everyone arrive and not sit down. During this standing meeting we spend five minutes sharing how God has been at work in the life of the congregation. We practice with each other sharing those outcomes in a way that is motivational and not just informational. Then, each council member gets two names and phone numbers and spends the next ten minutes making two five-minute phone calls to members. They thank the members for their financial gifts and tell the stories of impact that are taking place as a result of those gifts to empower the ministry of the congregation. This type of practice in telling the story helps us communicate the story more broadly in the congregation and teaches the leaders how to tell that story.

We need to recognize that we control our story until someone else controls it for us. Again, we need to teach current and former council members how to tell the story of their council service in a manner that inspires others to want to be part of this leadership opportunity. And if people are not honored and inspired by their time of service, we need to invite them to find other ways to use their gifts.

MEETING EVALUATION

Evaluate every meeting and be honest. Ask, Was the purpose of the meeting clearly set? Were people prepared? Did we have what we needed to make decisions? Did we learn how our ministry is making an impact? Did the ministry make progress toward our goal? Are we still aligned with our mission? Did anyone seem to have a personal agenda? And in all of this evaluation, have a sense of honesty with one another. Too often council members will quickly agree that the meeting fulfilled expectations in order to keep everyone happy, but then, in the parking lot after the meeting, they share what they really think.

VIEW COMMUNICATION THROUGH THE LENS OF YOUR DONORS

Review your communications from a donor perspective. The church worship bulletin is a fantastic place to cultivate donors who want to be more involved with your ministry. Here are some rewritten announcements that can help you evaluate your messaging and convert that messaging to meaningful, outcome-based interaction with your donors. Having the council lead this effort will help it permeate throughout the culture of the organization and show that the message is not simply being driven by the staff or communication team.

This announcement is from a bulletin in North Carolina.

2019 LYO Assembly

We are going to register for LYO Assembly soon. The theme for this year's assembly is "**This is Me**," and it will be held at the Embassy Suites in Greensboro, North Carolina. Cost for the event is $80 and includes all meals starting on Saturday. Please sign up on the youth room window or in Sunday School if you are interested in going. *Sign up is due TODAY*. Friends are welcome.

This is a pretty typical announcement. Let's look at it more closely and ask some questions.

- Would all who read this bulletin announcement understand the initials "LYO"?

- Who is the audience? If it is a "friend" with no knowledge, can you answer the impact expected from the event? Why would a parent send their child? Does anything good happen for youth housed in hotels?

- Note that the age group of possible attendees is not identified. That is important information.

- Is there enough information about the theme or details of the event to encourage anyone to invite a friend to this?

Here is a rewritten version that I suggest.

FIVE-HUNDRED DANCING YOUTH

Our youth will join five-hundred youth from across North Carolina to celebrate faith, live in community, and explore who we are as God's children. We attend Lutheran Youth Organization (LYO) each year because our youth committee has seen the long-term faith impact of this event on our own youth who are now in college. Recent graduate Sharon Smith has this to say about her experience: "The memories I have of attending LYO stay with me. It was there that I first felt like God would never let me go. I think about that often as I'm at college. Thanks for making that opportunity available to me." Cost is $80. Sign up today.

In this version of the announcement:

- An outcome story is shared from a college student. This also means someone has been in touch with her. This tells donors that we care for all our members, even those in college. It also tells donors that what we do has a long-term impact.

- The information shared lets our parents and kids know that we expect God to do something in the event.

- People see that this event fits into a larger plan for the youth committee to have a lasting impact on the faith lives of our youth.

Here is a traditional bulletin announcement about a special service.

Epiphany Vespers

Sunday, January 6 at 6:30 p.m. (following the chili cookoff)

"And they knelt down and paid him homage. Then, opening their treasure chest, they offered him gifts of gold, frankincense, and myrrh." (Matt 2:11)

Join us as we read and sing about the revelation of Jesus Christ to the gentiles and to all nations. Music will be led by Adult Choir and Jubilate Choir.

Nursery care will be provided.

My questions about this notice include the following.

- What is Epiphany? What are vespers? Why lead with that?

- Why does anyone come to this? What need does it fulfill for those who participate?

- Who do you think this notice is for? Will this stimulate someone who has never attended to come this year?

- Does this announcement make a donor feel like the organization just does stuff, or does it have a purpose behind its activity?

Instead, how about this?

I Recognized God Here

"I never see God as clearly as I do during the Epiphany Vespers service. *Epiphany* means to 'make known,' and as we share stories of where God is in our daily lives, I am so amazed at how God is still so active in our world." —Jim Starnes

During the Epiphany Vespers, we sing, and several people come prepared to tell stories of God's activity in the world. Join us to hear our choirs sing and your fellow members tell their stories of God's activity in their lives. Join us January 6 at 6:30 p.m. If you have any friends wondering where God is in the world, bring them, and it will become very clear to them.

How can your council and staff listen in a new way to its messages to ensure they reflect what we are really about? At a church I attended one Sunday, the pastor said, "We have worship on Wednesdays during Lent with a soup supper prior to worship. Let me tell you, the soup was excellent. I think I tried five different varieties last week."

From this announcement, you would think the focus of the Lenten gathering is on soup! The pre-Lenten worship gathering around the table with good soup can be meaningful as people talk about their lives and perhaps even share faith stories. But I would have liked the announcement to be more focused on outcomes. I wish the announcement had sounded more like this:

> We worship on Wednesdays during Lent because this is the time that we remember the journey Jesus made to the cross for us. This is a special time of worship in our life to remember that we are not alone, particularly during the difficulties of our life here on earth. We know your lives are busy, so we offer a simple soup supper so that you can feed your body even as you come to have your soul fed. Jack, one of our high school youth, had this to say about last week's service: "This is a busy time of year at school, but coming to worship last week really helped me put some things I'm dealing with at school in perspective. And the conversation I had with Bill and Sarah over dinner really made me feel like I have people here who care deeply about me." Join us Wednesday to take some time out of the craziness of your life to reflect on God's journey with us.

The council is called to see that the mission of the congregation is lived out. Let's see to it that the mission is what we communicate and are about. Not only will our ministries thrive, but I believe we will be more fulfilled by our time in leadership and governance for our congregations. As we communicate a thriving ministry that lives out its mission, congregation members will see the abundance of impact that living out our mission has on the people in the congregation and the ways they can impact our communities and the world.

CHAPTER 12.

WITNESS TO GENEROSITY

If field bees don't tell other bees where the good pollen or nectar source is, new bees would waste critical time looking for a good source when one has already been found. Bees don't keep these great sources a secret. In fact they are adamant about sharing with other potential foragers where to go so that time isn't wasted. The average bee only lives three weeks outside the hive. That isn't much time to get it right for the sake of the colony, so they share.

The week after I accepted the position to run the capital campaign for the camps in North Carolina, it was announced that a family made the lead gift of $750,000 we needed to build the first key project of the appeal. A few months later, our staff made their commitments, and a housekeeper pledged to give $5 per week for three years, or $780. Later in the campaign, a high school youth member of a congregation announced her intention to give up the soft drink she purchased each week at the convenience store. What she saved would be enough to provide a gift of $180 to the campaign. Like field bees returning to the hive to share the location of the pollen or nectar source, we shared these stories of generosity to stimulate the generosity of thousands of others who cared about our ministry.

SHARING STORIES

How do we learn anything if not by sharing our stories? When I was in the parish, I would ask my confirmation students how much their parents chose to give to the church during the most recent stewardship drive. It was fun to watch their faces when I would ask this. When they didn't know the answer, I would go on to ask how their parents made their giving decisions. Again, no response. If parents don't teach their kids how to be generous, how will they learn? So, I wrote my salary on the board. At that time we were giving 10 percent (we have grown since then), and I showed them the math. They were shocked anyone would talk about such things. Personally, I don't understand why we wouldn't.

One word of caution here. I don't share that story so that the older generations say something like, "Well, if only these parents today would teach their children about generosity, everything would be good financially in the church." The reality is that today's parents are following the model of their parents, who learned it from their parents. So, let's not blame anyone. Let's work to change the situation.

In my work, I have been privileged to get to know some of the most generous people in the United States. These aren't famous people but rather just solid, faithful, generous people. One story of generosity that I heard from a former colleague has had a huge impact on me. A particular couple was not giving as much financially as they thought was appropriate for their leadership role in the church. So, they covenanted with one another to grow by 1 percent per year in their giving and never stop. They reached 38 percent before Bob passed away.

Another one of the most generous people I knew lived by himself on a very busy street in Charleston, South Carolina. I remember the first time I visited in his humble home and wondering if he could really be making the gifts that he was giving. One day he called me and said that he had seen our list of needs published in the camp newsletter. He told me he could take care of funding the list, which included a new minivan for our day camp teams to use. I have been inspired by his generosity ever since this encounter.

GIVING IS A STATEMENT OF FAITH

Giving money away is a statement of faith. It is a declaration that God has provided all that we have and that what we have is enough. We will live like the flowers in the field that are referenced in Matthew 6:28–30, which don't worry about tomorrow. This statement of faith should be something that we are willing to talk about.

My goal is for every Christian to grow in their generosity all the time. Everyone can grow in generosity. Sometimes, due to life circumstances, that could mean giving away less money, such as when one is going through medical treatment or a divorce. Other times, it could mean giving differently, such as giving a base amount plus a percentage of a bonus or windfall. Or it could mean including the church in your estate plans for a percentage of what is left after you are gone.

People who have discovered generosity have come to understand God as a God of abundance. They have not bought in to the idea that there isn't enough, but rather they believe that what they have is a gift, and the gift should be shared. It is through their witness that culture begins to change in our congregations. This witness lets others know that it is okay to struggle with generosity, and it is okay to try and fail. As we witness to our giving, we help others discover the ways in which they can be generous and live to reflect the abundance that we have in our lives.

A STUDY IN GENEROSITY

I have written a small-group study that can be completed in fifteen, thirty, or sixty minutes depending on how much time the small group has to devote to it. It includes an introduction to giving and why we give, and how it is that we don't give.

The key discussion guide includes the following.

- Ask everyone in the group to share their answers to the following questions with at least one other person.
    - Who is the most generous person you have known in your life? Please share a story about how you witnessed their generosity.
    - What is the first financial gift you remember ever giving? To whom did you give it, how much was it, and why did you choose to make this gift?
- Ask people to share the best of their responses with the entire group.

- Have people share their answers to these questions with someone else in the group.
  - How has your giving to the church grown throughout your life? How is it that you continue to grow in your giving?
  - Why do you give financially to the church?
- Share the best responses with the entire group.
- As a large group, ask people to share their responses to the following questions.
  - How does giving to the church make you feel?
  - What would you share with a new member as to the importance of them being generous in their financial participation in the church?
  - What excites you most about the future of our congregation?
  - What is your biggest hope for the congregation to accomplish once the *stewardship* appeal is concluded?
- Conclude by sharing that the purpose of the stewardship appeal is that we each become more generous, and together we will achieve our goals.
- Take a minute to answer questions people have.

If you would like the entire piece, visit GSBFR.com, and click the link for the small-group study.

My other favorite activity for year-round generosity sharing is to include a monthly story in the congregation's newsletter or to do a video interview once per month with a person or couple in the congregation, sharing how they learned to be generous and continue to seek to be generous. These statements of faith can inspire peers to grow in their generosity.

I have often encouraged confirmation students to interview their parents and other adults to capture these stories as well. Confirmation students learn from these interviews and help hold adults accountable to grow in their generosity since they have the responsibility to be faith mentors. The piece also encourages people to understand that generosity is not a destination but a journey. Those being interviewed need to know that they do not have to be perfect models of generosity. The goal of the interview is to lift up the idea that growing in generosity is the faithful response.

You will notice that I only talk about generosity and growth in generosity, and am not focused on the size of gifts. I certainly love major gifts, but the premise of this book is that all of us can be generous according to our means and grow in generosity. This is open to all of us, no matter our wealth.

How do you discover the stories of generosity in your congregation? Sometimes, you can look at the numbers and discover that there must be a story behind them. This happens when you see that someone grew from $200 per year to $2,400 per year in their intended giving. It can also happen when you intentionally ask people.

In a Detroit suburb, following a very successful annual appeal that saw intended giving increase by $3,000 per week for the coming year, we decided to gather a sample of the congregation. We invited fifteen people who fit one of the following categories:

- They grew by a significant percentage.
- They were already generous and grew further.
- They were new to the congregation and became a leading donor family very quickly.

Of the fifteen people we invited, thirteen attended the gathering where we told them we would evaluate the recent stewardship drive and learn from them about their generosity journey. Those who attended ranged in age from thirty-five to eighty and reflected the diversity that was present in the congregation.

When asked about how they learned generosity, this group overwhelmingly pointed to people in their lives who demonstrated generosity to them. In some cases, they learned generosity growing up through the witness of parents and grandparents, but more critical for them was the witness of those who are in their lives today. One shared that he isn't very generous, but he married a great person who teaches him by example every day. Another mentioned a coworker who gives sacrificially to her students. Another mentioned the witness of the pastor who was very open about his relationship with material possessions. This group did know the theological and biblical stories that point to generosity, but for them the most powerful witness was people they know and love living by example and sharing their own generosity.

Until I heard the story of the couple who covenanted to grow by 1 percent per year and never stop, I did not realize that giving more than 10 percent was really something people did. Since then, I have learned of people giving 50 percent away, and I know of one couple who is living a reverse tithe: they live on 10 percent and give away 90 percent. I'm not lifting these witnesses up as a model for what we are to do. I simply lift them up as people who have demonstrated their generosity to me and therefore impact how it is that my family seeks to become more generous as we journey through life.

In order to lead a congregation to a culture of generosity, we have to witness to that generosity. Witnessing isn't bragging about giving money away. It is teaching others about our faith in God, which leads us to not hold on to everything we have. Instead, we learn to live as if God is creator and that everything we have is a gift of God. And we have to make the connection of faith and generosity. Being able to give money away is a statement of belief that God will provide. God will provide not because you gave money away, but because that is just what God does. It is through witnessing to generosity that we begin to see the full scope of the abundance that God provides in this world because we see it from a perspective beyond just our own.

We need to act like the older bees in the hive and teach the new bees how to be generous. If we don't share our story, no one can learn from our history, and everyone will be left to fend for themselves. To achieve abundance and generosity, our witness to what we have learned is critical to leading others to join us and perpetuating this value.

CHAPTER 13

$10,000 CARWASH: SPECIAL APPEALS FROM AN ABUNDANCE MENTALITY

As a beekeeper, I can engage a few tactics to increase honey production. One manipulation is to add a capped brood (baby bees that will hatch within a week) into a hive about two weeks prior to when the best nectar-producing flowers are about to bloom. This gives more bees in the hive the opportunity to receive nectar from the foragers and allows more of the house bees to start flying sooner to collect nectar. This effectively increases the honey yield. This past year I harvested seventy-three gallons of honey.

Sometimes, fundraising efforts require creative, large-scale tactics to produce needed results. Just as introducing a brood of hatchling bees to a hive stimulates an increased honey yield, introducing a game-changing tactic into our stewardship efforts is sometimes required.

For example, let's think about youth ministry in our congregations. Statistics tell us that the average youth ministry professional lasts about sixteen to eighteen months in their job before they burn out and quit. I think the number one reason for this is that we make them fundraise to support their ministry. Not only that, we ask them to do this fundraising by using ineffective methods that reinforce a scarcity mentality. I was once part of a forty-two–week fundraiser for a national youth event that was based on the youth collecting change each week. You guessed it; they never secured enough to get there, and they proved to everyone there wasn't enough.

When I was a youth, my youth director sold my services to a member of the congregation for yard work to help me raise money to get to camp. His gift amounted to $2 per hour. At the time, my personal lawn business was charging close to $10 per hour. I would have been better off getting another yard to mow on my own and fending for myself.

I have seen youth do car washes and end up with about $100 if they are lucky. A youth group Easter breakfast pulled in a lot of $3 per plate "gifts" for the youth group. Besides, who really thinks it is a good idea to get the youth group up at 4:00 a.m. on Easter morning to cook eggs and expect them to give service with a smile?!

The problem with these fundraising activities is that they have no ministry value to the kids or the congregation. We may share a bit of information, like where we are going and what it will cost, but rarely do these events share why we are going and what we expect God to do through the program or the event. Furthermore, we don't invite the donor on the journey with us.

CLARIFY THE WHY

As I have said in earlier chapters, I believe that the reasons we are doing fundraising events must always begin with the outcomes we are hoping to realize. Whether we do breakfasts or car washes, why we are doing the fundraising should be emphasized. People will give to youth fundraisers, but they will give more if you can provide clear and inspiring outcome stories about what God is doing through the youth or through the trip. For instance, find a previous participant who is now in college to come back (or send a selfie video) sharing the impact that such an event has on her faith life. She has carried this experience with her to college, and she is excited that the next generation of youth get to participate in the event that meant so much to her. Have the youth share what they expect God to do in their lives through the event. Have the youth director share why the event is part of their youth ministry plan and how they expect the kids to grow as a result of it.

SHARE A GIFT CHART

Then, ask people for the size gifts you *really* need. If you need $15,000, share a gift chart such as the one below so the congregation knows what you need:

Number of gifts needed	Amount of gift	Running total
1	$1,500	$1,500
2	$1,000	$3,500
4	$500	$5,500
12	$300	$10,100
25	$125	$13,225
28	$60	$14,905
Many	Other amounts	$15,000

A special appeal such as this should not last more than six weeks, regardless of how much money is being sought. Furthermore, the number one reason a special appeal will fail is because not enough people participate, so utilize challenge gifts and other tactics to increase your response. Always keep the focus on the outcome of the ministry that you are seeking. As I've said earlier, if we simply inform and then ask without motivating, people will think their money is all we are after. The model I seek to implement makes the fundraising activity a part of the ministry. By having former participants share the impact of a similar event, you are continuing their faith journey. By having the kids discern their hopes for what God will do through the event, you are making them more aware that you expect them to consider how God will impact them as part of the event. By having the youth director establish goals for the event ensures that there is deep purpose to what you are doing. All of this enhances the ministry value of the experience, and it raises more money.

My vision is that the fundraising event be seen as an integral part of the ministry, not a necessary evil to stage before the real ministry can begin. I also believe that fundraising activities should be about enough money to do the ministry with excellence. People want to be part of meaningful ministry and will rise to new levels of giving to make it happen.

When I was in the parish, we launched a plan for a mission trip. We set a goal to raise significantly more money than we needed for the group to go so that we could invest significantly in the community we would be visiting and serving. We didn't worry that there were not enough financial resources to make the trip a reality. We had confidence people would be even more excited when we had the opportunity to have a bigger impact.

Special gift appeals also allow us to demonstrate great

leadership. Whatever committee or group would be most interested in a project should be provided the opportunity to give first. Encourage their connection to the project by asking them to lead with their gifts. And we don't start asking others to give until we have 100 percent of this group supporting the project at the level they are able to support it. We also seek leadership gifts from people who have the most passion for this particular project. Often this is not the largest givers to the congregation. These special appeals raise up significant new donors as these appeals align with their passions.

When we launch a special appeal with the confidence that we can reach our goal and deploy tactics that inform, motivate, and ask in an effective manner, our appeals can lead to abundance rather than feeling like there isn't enough. When the fundraising activity points more toward the ministry taking place and the impact of the ministry rather than the fundraising event itself, a culture of abundance begins to permeate what we are about. When the fundraising event feels like ministry itself, we have begun to achieve our goal of a culture of generosity in our congregation.

CHAPTER 14.

A DIFFERENT STORY AS THE CHURCH: STEWARDSHIP FOR ALL SEASONS

In the early 2000s honeybee colonies were dying at an alarming rate. In fact, in the United States feral bee colonies living on their own in the wild no longer exist. Mites, disease, pesticides, monoculture farming, and a whole host of other environmental factors have made it very difficult on the bees. Two years ago, one of my beekeeping mentors lost 75 percent of his hives. I lost over 50 percent. It is a hard time to keep bees. However, there are some very promising new tactics. Some of these don't require chemicals, while others utilize chemicals that naturally occur in the hive already to control mites and other problems. Just because it has become hard to keep bees doesn't mean we should stop. And we are astute enough to know that doing things the way we used to do them is not the right way to go. We pay attention to what is working and what isn't, and we believe that better days are ahead. This year, 75 percent of my hives made it through the winter.

Successful beekeeping requires constant attention. Utilizing one single tactic is not enough. A variety of tactics need to be applied through the year. In the same way, I believe we need to be thinking of stewardship as an ongoing aspect of ministry. We need to think of steward-ship "for all seasons."

We are all familiar with the annual stewardship drive, which has been around for a long time. Some congregations have given up on it, but others conduct the drive without expecting significant results. Low expectations lead to being satisfied when people give the same year over year so that no substantial cuts need to be made. Others intentionally hold the budget flat and move the pastor to part-time status. Others chase the trendy new way of raising money and assume it will fix the system.

Our experience as a consulting firm is different. My partner, Richard Sayther, has written a program called Stewardship for All Seasons (SAS), which he developed by applying to the congregational setting what we learned from helping other nonprofit institutions in their development work. This program focuses on the processes you have been reading about here. We begin with case development followed by an intentional time of informing, motivating, asking, and thanking. The case is built around our mission and vision and how much new money will be needed next year for new ministry to implement that mission and vision.

What changes each year is what new money is needed as part of the strategic plan. What doesn't change is starting with case development and cultivating and asking donors for gifts. The time between informing and asking is spent sharing outcome stories and implementing our goals and initiatives for how we will impact the world with the good news. We stop talking about shrinking budgets and focus more on what we can and will do.

The average congregation working with SAS grows by 15 percent in the first year, whether they are urban, suburban, rural, inner city, or located in some other context. The reason it works is that people in our churches are hungry to hear about what God is doing in the world and what we plan to continue to do in the future. It isn't gimmicky. It treats every member like the person they are and asks them to join in making the ministry a reality.

It is our belief that congregations with vital missions and a strong sense of how they want to accomplish that mission will double their gifted revenue every seven years. This happens through current members growing their generosity and the congregation reaching new people because they suddenly know the story to share with their neighbors to help the ministry grow. Good stewardship can lead to strong evangelism because it is about discerning stories of what God is up to in your community.

CHANGING CONGREGATIONAL CULTURE

Through Stewardship for All Seasons, we are seeking to change the culture in our congregations from one of scarcity to one of abundance. Again, abundance is a mindset and not a condition of wealth. Abundance recognizes that God is the God of the first article of the creed, has created us and all that exists, and provides all that we need.

It takes tenacity to change the culture of a congregation. When a congregation never increases revenue, people believe that there isn't enough. When the facility is not cared for, people feel there isn't enough. When we continue to ask for money each week and never tell people the impact that previous gifts have, people feel there isn't enough. When we are just about information and never about outcome, people think we just want their money.

Cultural change takes diligent work. It takes education, spiritual growth, and living out your mission and inviting people into that.

Congregations with a strong culture of stewardship combine engaged pastor and staff leadership with a strong core of lay leaders. Together and throughout the whole year, this leadership team works to help everyone experience abundance in their lives and help people to articulate that this is what is happening in their lives.

The default in our society is to avoid talking about generosity and giving. That's one of the factors that makes it hard to change congregation culture into a culture of abundance. I cannot stress enough that changing culture requires continuous attention and care. I'm amazed at the number of congregations that will pay to journey with us for a year, but the pastor quits attending meetings after revenue increases by 15 percent. I am glad congregations are happy with the results, but I am concerned when their attention turns to the next thing that they can spend their time on. They will have more money but may not have a real change in culture.

Ministry is more fulfilling as the culture changes around stewardship. Not only do you accomplish more, but you focus more on what God is doing than on the busyness of ministry. It is fulfilling to hear the stories of ministry outcomes. Below you will find some outcomes described by those who have journeyed in SAS with me.

From Pastor Kim Carlson, Good Shepherd, Elizabeth City, North Carolina:

> Good Shepherd is a small congregation (average worship attendance of sixty-two people) situated just outside a rural town, Elizabeth City, in eastern North Carolina. Established in the early 2000s, Good Shepherd suffered a sig-

nificant congregational decline after moving into their ministry center in 2010. Combined with its high debt load, this decline threatened to put the congregation in serious jeopardy.

The SAS program helped us realize that the work of good financial stewardship starts long before the beginning of the annual fall stewardship appeal and continues long after the pledges have been handed in. Using the principles Mike taught us, Good Shepherd has met its goals for increased giving for the past three years in a row. This program helped us balance our budget for the first time since moving into our ministry center in 2010, fund a variety of growing ministries, and weather the economic challenge we faced when our largest donor unexpectedly died.

Obviously, the return we have received on our investment in the Stewardship for all Seasons program has been substantial, and we are thankful for the difference it has made at Good Shepherd. As a pastoral leader, my dread of the annual fall stewardship appeal has been transformed into a time when I have the opportunity to share our congregation's hopes and visions for the future along with the financial backing needed to turn vision into reality.

From Pastor Paul Walters, Lutheran Church of the Master, Troy, Michigan:

LCM is located in an upper-middle-class suburb of Detroit and composed of a significant number of auto industry engineers as well as doctors and nurses. LCM also has a history of peace and is able to laugh together, which is a gift. There are two important stories to tell about the positive changes Stewardship for All Seasons has brought to the financial life of the congregation.

In 2013 the church took on the challenge of a capital campaign to renovate outdated bathrooms and refresh the narthex. The cost was to be around $140,000. The congregation voted to move forward with the project and began pledging toward it. People were invited to make commitments of up to three years in length, and no specific goals were made. At the end of construction, the congregation had to take out a loan for around $30,000. This was paid off well ahead of schedule, and in the end, excess funds created a building fund of some $15,000. All in all, a good outcome. Or so we thought.

In 2017 the church worked with Mike Ward's guidance on a second capital appeal. In this case the goal was $80,000 to replace aging HVAC equipment and replace an outdoor sign. Prior to bringing the proposal to the congregation, pledges totaling $20,000 were secured. In the end, within three weeks the congregation received over $90,000 in gifts and pledges. Not only was the initial work completed, but a second project was taken on and $5,000 given away to a local nonprofit.

As a leader this meant I had to seek out those initial gifts. It meant having conversations with people about money and directly asking for support. At first these conversations were not easy, but I have found people actually appreciate being asked. They also love to hear stories of how their gifts have inspired others.

In a similar way, our annual stewardship appeal has changed. Now each year we focus on specific new or enhanced ministry goals with specific financial goals. In 2018, for the first time ever, we had a challenge grant of $5,000 to help move from 106 pledging units to 120 units. Before the campaign was complete, an unsolicited second $5,000 was contributed toward the challenge grant, and 126 units were pledged.

In addition, because of the strong support of our ministry goals, pledges to the annual fund increased by nearly 10 percent for a total of $40,000.

The focus on planning for the future and setting clear ministry goals has been a gift. This helps form an agenda for council meetings throughout the year. It serves as a reminder that we are called to continue to innovate, try new things, and take risks to share the good news of Jesus. Best of all, this means the ministry drives the money, not the other way around.

We thought we were doing pretty well with our stewardship program here at LCM. It turns out we were only just beginning. Working with Stewardship for All Seasons has opened up new opportunities for ministry, and our congregation and community will be blessed in countless ways.

From Ben Keseley, Saint George's Episcopal Church, Arlington, Virginia:

Saint George's is an ethnically and demographically diverse congregation just outside of downtown Washington, DC. By nature of our location we are a transient parish. Our family structures, economic situations, sexual orientations, and geographic origins are a representation of what you will find in the DC area.

During and following a capital campaign for renovation, our annual ministry fund was falling short of reaching our needs, and we were living off of our reserve funds. As we got closer and closer to the day those reserves would be gone, we contacted Mike and looked into Stewardship for All Seasons.

We had conducted our normal fall stewardship drive before working with Mike and had pledges in hand from most of our families. For the first time ever, with Mike's guidance, we launched something we called the "Generosity Journey" and went back to each family asking them to increase their giving by a specific amount to help us close our projected shortfall of over $100,000. For us, this was very new and a bit uncomfortable.

However, our vestry and generosity team led the way with 100 percent participation among their members and secured a challenge gift to motivate the parish. Saint Georgians responded by being invited to join the vestry and generosity team in their leadership. People of all ages and backgrounds stepped up as they realized we could no longer live off reserves. Cutting staff and expenses was not of interest to us. We were determined to maintain the levels of ministry that we valued as a parish. Through the parish's generosity, we reached our financial goal.

The Generosity Journey happened in March. We

launched our regular appeal again the following fall, rein-forcing our ask that what people did in the Generosity Journey became their new baseline level of giving. We asked them to again increase their giving to allow us to fully fund our facility care and social ministry needs. The congrega-tion again stepped up. Our revenue has gone from $590,000 when we started with Mike to a projection of $720,000 this year. This increase spans less than a two-year period of time.

At the same time, as the result of a significant bequest, we were able to launch a campaign to purchase a new pipe organ and make necessary renovations and acoustical enhancements to our nave in order to accommodate the new instrument. With major gift and targeted fundraising underway, we have already raised over $1.2 million of our $1.6 million goal from just thirty-three families. We are highly confident in the remainder of our campaign and wait with great anticipation and excitement for our new instru-ment to arrive in the fall of 2020.

Our culture is shifting from one of not having enough to recognizing that we can accomplish what we set our minds to, and Saint Georgians are people who are eager to keep our ministry strong, vibrant, and moving forward. What could have been a period of entrenchment and cutbacks has turned into a period of thriving and advancing. A time of grateful generosity.

I am very excited about sharing these stories because they help illustrate the importance of committing to steward-ship as work that must go on through all seasons, every year.

In today's world, it could be easy to say that the church is on the decline and that is simply the reality. Just as honeybee colony management is more difficult because of mites, so too life in the congregation is harder and decline is inevitable. However, there are new approaches. Changing tactics on treating mites is working. So too,

SAS is a tactic working for stewardship in our congregations. We need to be open to figuring out how to be effective today in the reality of life as the church.

CHAPTER 15.

GROWING GIVERS' HEARTS

In late fall, all of the male bees (drones) are killed by the female worker bees. The reason for this is that drones have one job and that is to fertilize the queen. Each queen goes on one mating flight, and once mated, she lives in the hive for the rest of her life unless she swarms with half the hive to start a new colony. Once a colony knows that the queen they have is fertile and will be the one that gets them through the winter, there is no longer a need for the drones, since all they would do is eat honey throughout the winter and offer nothing of value to the hive. Therefore, on "drone assassination day," as I call it, they are dispatched. When the colony needs more drones in the spring, the queen will lay drone eggs and produce more at that time.

Bee colonies obviously go to extreme lengths to protect the hive and to ensure its survival. Of course, we value all people in our congregations, from the smallest giver to the largest. We are not in the habit of lopping people from their roles for giving less than their perceived fair share. But we do need to take stock on a regular basis of giving patterns and take action to grow the hearts of all our givers, no matter where they are in their giving journey. To really grow givers' hearts, we need a long-term stewardship plan for our donors based on where they are.

I won't address the many nuances of growing a major donor in this chapter. That will be the topic of a future book and blog posts that can be found on our website. For this book, I want to focus on four different types of donors.

FIRST-TIME DONORS

For a nonprofit institution, a first-time donor is like gold. Effective nonprofits understand the lifetime value such a donor brings to the organization. They know from predictive modeling how a donor can grow over time to become a major supporter of a ministry. The work of cultivating that relationship begins the moment the first check arrives at the organization. Many nonprofits even provide special packets to first-time donors as well as procedures for follow-up to ensure the best chance of receiving a second gift.

Please don't be the congregation that ignores first-time donors. Being aware of first-time givers is extremely important. I know of very few pastors who are alerted to a first-time gift received by the congregation. Fewer still send a thank-you note in the first twenty-four hours after receiving a gift, and fewer follow up in any significant way to let the donor know the impact that their gift has made. We need to build a strategy with tactics to reach out to new givers.

When I was in the parish, the pastor I worked with would give me a list of visitors and ask me to follow up with them. I will admit at that time in my life, cold calling people was not my favorite activity. If my first call was to someone who was really perturbed that I interrupted their dinner, I often found excuses not to make the next calls on my list. However, if my list had indicated those who had already made their first financial contribution, I would have started with those donors and feel quite confident the engagement would have been far greater with those who had already chosen to be financially active in the congregation.

Congregations need to develop protocol for thanking people for their giving. First off, it is the right thing to do. Second, if someone financially supports the congregation, it shows they are interested. Remember, Jesus says that "where your treasure is, your heart will be also." That means that once people make a first-time gift, we have a bit of their heart. I believe we then become responsible to see if we can encourage more of their heart to be attached to the congregation. The first gift is the donor flirting with the organization. It is up to the organization to have a plan for seeing if the donor wants to move the relationship to the next level.

NEW MEMBERS

When we joined our current congregation, we had a two-hour orientation session. We were taught a little theology, learned a little about the history of the congregation, got to know the other new members, and then got "the talk." Well, sort of. I remember it being pretty awkward. The leader of the orientation session simply told us that the white envelopes were for our annual fund gifts, and the green envelopes were for the building fund. We were not told how those funds were really used or the impact that the gifts in either envelope were making.

We did give. We gave because we were very excited about the ministry we were joining. Our daughter would be in the preschool, and that was convenient for our family. Worship was high quality, and the pastor was an excellent teacher and preacher. We had chosen this congregation and were happy to become part of it.

I believe there is no better time to ask someone for a gift than at the time they have chosen to join you. But that ask should include a description of how those gifts will be used to carry out the vision and mission of the congregation. As new members we did not know the congregation's cultural norms relating to how giving was handled. We would have welcomed any information. Again, we were choosing to join *them*. I think we sometimes fear that we will run people off if we talk about giving when they join. In reality, asking for gifts and telling them why their giving is important is a crucial first step to growing the hearts of our newest members.

Seize the opportunity, but don't simply ask for money. Go through the cycle—Inform, Motivate, Ask, and then Thank. At the time of joining, give people a sense of the needs and goals of the congregation. Bring people into the recent accomplishments. Show them what goals you are funding this year with new money. Then, let them know that since their money is new money, it will be funding your new initiatives. Finally, make sure people are sharing motivational stories of the congregation, and let the new members motivate one another by sharing what excites them about the new congregation.

I have often encountered this question related to new members: How do we know how much to ask them to contribute? It is difficult when you have no giving history, but you can consider the following options for addressing the question of how much new members should consider giving.

- Provide statistics that show the average gift and median gift for the congregation. Take care to say that this is simply a guide.

- Listen to their story, and ask about what aspects of ministry they are most passionate about. This can help both you and them begin to imagine the best levels of giving.

- You may even ask new members to describe their giving journey without asking for specific numbers. Hearing their stories may also help them think about how they want to connect their giving dollars to your congregation's ministry and give you clues about the best ask for each person. Remember, people like to be asked, and when they are joining your ministry is a time in their life that they are very excited about that ministry being strong and impactful into the future.

Pretending they don't want to give or fearing you will offend them is just off base. When someone joins, it is the best time to cultivate and ask.

LAPSED DONORS

There is a term in the fundraising world called LYBUNT (Last Year but Unfortunately Not This Year). It is important to communicate with your LYBUNTs and monitor their giving pattern. If someone typically gives all of their financial support in December, it is a good idea to communicate with them each December to invite them to renew their giving. It is also important to respect the way in which they do give and help them to grow from that point.

It is also important to monitor an organization's LYBUNT donors and react based on their history. If we have a donor who normally gives in March but didn't give this year, we should not assume they will never give again. Many donors forget or change their habits due to tax situations or other commitments. If we simply assume they will never give to you again, there is a good chance that will become a self-fulfilling prophecy.

I have heard stories of couples thinking the other was writing the checks. There are plenty of stories about people forgetting their contributions. So, do them a favor, and ask about it. You will not offend people by contacting them. In fact, you will let them know that your ministry is really important and that you are paying attention.

SMALL DONORS

Donors of smaller amounts can feel that their gifts don't make a difference if we aren't careful. They can feel like they get lost in the shuffle as we celebrate challenge gifts, legacy gifts, and lead gifts. In order to grow a smaller donor into a generous donor, we need to thank them just as we do others. We also need to express how important they are to the mission of the congregation and help them recognize they have the capacity to grow in their giving. One of the greatest ways to help a donor grow is by inviting them to give regular, recurring gifts. Often automatic giving through electronic options will help a smaller donor grow to a medium-sized donor.

I once had a potential donor tell me that they could not give $1,000 to a capital campaign over three years. So, I asked them for $1 per day. As we talked, they shared that $1 per day would be pretty easy. He mentioned that he spent $4.60 per day at Starbucks and had no idea what that added up to over time. This donor ended up making a $3,000 gift to the campaign. The value of regular, recurring gifts is critical for helping people make a larger contribution.

Many congregations have found intentional recruitment to automatic giving to be very helpful. Sometimes a challenge donor is found who will provide a special gift of $100 to the congregation for every new family that enrolls in automatic giving. I have seen a congregation in Virginia grow by fifty-three new families enrolled in a single year. Another congregation was able to offer $20,000 in matching money for pledged increases from their donors who gave on average less than $10 per week. They received over $16,000 of the match, which provided tremendous growth from this often forgotten giving category. This group made a major step forward on their generosity journey.

TRACKING DONOR GROWTH

It is important to track donor giving patterns. You won't know if your donors are growing in their giving or if they have growth potential if you are not tracking giving on a donor-by-donor basis. Here is an example of three donors whose giving we tracked year over year.

Donor 1 increased from $416 to $1,820.
Donor 2 increased from $52 to $572.
Donor 3 increased from $156 to $884.

If we look at people on a generosity journey, the three donors listed above are moving nicely from being small donors to being regular donors and perhaps to even more significant givers. Imagine what God must be doing in their lives to grow in one case by more than 2,600 percent! As their pastor, I would desire to learn what is happening in their lives and to know what caused the change. I would want to find ways for them to tell their stories in order to mentor others in growth. I would also want to thank them and acknowledge that I have noticed their commitment and growth in their generosity journey.

As we grow the hearts of givers, we see the reflection in their lives of a God of abundance. People feel less like they are trapped in a world of scarcity and they begin to see God for all the blessings provided in their lives. Witnessing the growth in generosity in people and learning their stories of how they are seeing God active in their lives can be the most meaningful and rewarding part of engaging in stewardship ministry for leaders. This spiritual growth is at the core of what we are about as the church. It is less about money and more about people and their hearts.

Unlike the bee colony where useless bees are dispatched, we have the opportunity and honor to grow donors to deeper relationship with our churches.

CHAPTER 16.

SHOULD THE PASTOR KNOW?

If the bees were keeping secret from the queen how much pollen and honey were in the hive, the hive would die. Either the queen would lay too many eggs, and the colony would starve because there wouldn't be enough honey to sustain so many bees, or the colony would die because not enough new bees were being produced. For the hive to thrive, the leader needs to know what resources are available. When pollen is coming in, she can lay eggs because there is enough protein to sustain the new bees. When there is a dearth of pollen or nectar, she can slow down production so that the hive can remain healthy.

"Should the pastor know what people give?" This is the most frequently asked question I get from people trying to grow stewardship in their congregations. People are often afraid that someone will get upset if the pastor knows what people give. Some congregations celebrate that only one person, usually the financial secretary, knows what people give. Some fear that the pastor will treat the generous people better than the nongenerous. Much anxiety is wrapped up in this question.

Yes, I think the pastor should know what people give, though how that happens may not be a one-size-fits-all approach. I also think we need to clarify the difference between confidentiality and secrecy. In all these discussions, nobody ever asks, "Are people offended that the pastor has not acknowledged their generosity?" This makes me wonder if people need accountability in order to break free from their fears of truly being generous.

I think the bee colony can provide us a good example. Just as the leader of the hive needs to know the resources that are available, so too the leadership of the church can be far more effective when they know.

One of my favorite quotes about this comes from the Reverend Martin Luther King Sr. In one of his sermons he said, "The practice of anonymous giving leads to the practice of anonymous non-giving."[1] If there is no accountability for what people give, there is no reason people should challenge themselves to give more. Perhaps this is what has led Protestants giving to charity each year as a median percentage of less than 1 percent of their income.

At one time, it was the practice in my congregation to fill out a pledge form, stuff it in an envelope, and hand it over it to the church. The envelopes were collected, but nobody would open them. The envelopes were then mailed back to us in late spring the following year. Over time I realized this practice reinforced a mentality that giving was between God and me. It is true that giving is between God and me, but it also involves the whole congregation. The congregation needs to be able to talk about its dreams for new ministry. This is part of hearing God's voice in the conversation. Isn't the pastor who asks,

1. Ian S. Markham and Oren W. Warder, *An Introduction to Ministry: A Primer for Renewed Life and Leadership in Mainline Protestant Congregations* (Hoboken, NJ: Wiley, 2016), 229.

"Could you consider an extra $3 per week?" also part of the voice of God in this conversation? If we make the response a private commitment on a piece of paper that no one reads, we may mistake our voice for the voice of God in challenging us to consider growing in generosity.

Returning to the King quote, I would ask this: What is wrong with accountability? I remember in high school, I had an accountability partner that checked in with me regularly about my prayer life and my daily devotional habits. It helped me develop a discipline in those areas. We can teach people to develop a spiritual giving habit through accountability.

WHERE YOUR TREASURE IS

Jesus says in Matthew 6:21, "Where your treasure is, there your heart will be also." This teaches us that when we guide people into a practice of accountability about our giving, we are investing in the ministry of the church as a matter of the heart. I think pastors should be involved in the matters of the hearts of their members.

Giving patterns change in the lives of people when major activities take place in their lives. For example, a couple will often stop giving when they are considering a divorce. I would like the pastor to know about the marriage problems in order to refer the couple to counseling and to offer prayer before it is too late. If someone begins to have anxiety about a potential layoff, they often hold back on their giving. The pastor could provide care during such a time. People often feel guilty when financial circumstances dictate that they decrease their giving, and the pastor could have a role in alleviating that feeling of guilt. On the other hand, people often give a windfall gift when they get a promotion. I would like the pastor to be able to celebrate that event. Others increase giving when they pay off a major debt or come to a deeper understanding of God's presence in their lives. Again, these are activities the pastor should be aware of and respond to.

Recently, I had a conversation with a congregation where the pastor has historically not known what members give. One of their largest donors had not yet made a gift in the most recent year. In each of the previous two years, this particular member had provided over $12,000 each year. The pastor doesn't know who this donor is, so he doesn't have the capacity to have a conversation to find out if they are going to give this year, if they are upset, or if they simply forgot. By making the giving of donors transparent, we can equip the pastor to have a conversation with anyone about his or her giving. Much may be on the line. If a member who gives a large annual gift doesn't give this year, perhaps staffing will need to be addressed, including laying one or more people off. In order to function and thrive as a church, pastors need to know what people give.

Once when my wife and I had stretched to give the largest gift we had ever given to any organization, the pastor wrote a personal note on the thank-you letter. It impressed me that our generosity was appreciated. It is not the reason we give, but it is nice to be thanked.

There isn't a college president in America or leader of a charitable organization who doesn't know the giving history of their donors. Knowing this information helps leaders guide and strengthen their organization. Pastors are called to serve all members of the congregation, regardless of what they give. We need to trust our pastors will be strengthened, not discouraged by knowing more about congregation giving.

So yes, I think the pastor should know. Most generous people want the pastor to know, and many people are relieved when they can talk about money openly with their pastor. This goes for those with significant resources and those whose resources are limited. The traditions that favor anonymous giving need to change in our congregations. If your congregation follows this tradition of anonymity, I encourage you to take the lead in making a change to this policy. I want everyone in our congregations to give generously according to their means, and I know that it is unlikely that they will reach greater levels of generosity on their own. The human condition doesn't allow for it.

One relatively simple way to increase generosity is sharing donor information with the pastor. If your congregation currently does not do this but is ready to make the change to greater transparency, I don't suggest making a big deal about the transition. My favorite tactic is to have the pastor simply sign one of the quarterly statements in blue ink so that it is obvious that the pastor knows. I also suggest that the council president be informed that this change in practice is taking place. I do not recommend that this change in policy be debated and discussed, but if the tradition of anonymous giving is longstanding, you may need to discuss the advantages for making the change. Each pastor has their own style, and each congregation has their own dynamics that must be considered with an issue like this. Just because one or two people announce that they don't want the pastor to know, it doesn't mean they are correct. I believe many more people will thank the pastor and leadership for acknowledging their generosity and leading the congregation in the area of generosity.

THE STEWARDSHIP TEAM

In addition to the pastor, I believe that at least one member of the stewardship team should also be aware of the giving data in a congregation. Otherwise, too much burden is placed on the pastor to put the stewardship drive together. Ideally, the stewardship team member will be generous themselves and be fully aware of how to keep information confidential. This reminds me of what the apostle Paul writes in his first letter to the Corinthians: "Think of us in this way, as servants of Christ and stewards of God's mysteries. Moreover, it is required of stewards that they be found trustworthy" (1 Cor 4:1–2). When we lead stewardship in a trustworthy way, we invite others into open and loving community. As a congregation, we know who to call when we need a funeral meal provided or someone to schedule acolytes. This person on the stewardship team simply becomes who we call when we need to talk to people about money. It is part of our spiritual discipline. We need to stop hiding it behind a veil of secrecy. When we expand the circle to someone on the stewardship team, we raise the level of knowledge, which helps us be more effective in our asking people for their gifts. This change will be challenging for some. But addressing this challenge positively will lead the congregation to growth and new opportunities.

LIFTING THE VEIL OF SECRECY

In *Passing the Plate*, the authors put forth nine hypotheses about why American Christians are not more generous than they are. Three of these hypotheses are focused on the veil of secrecy regarding money, with one directly linked to the pastor knowing. The relevant hypotheses from Smith and Emerson are as follows.[2]

- "Low Leadership Expectations: American Christians do not give generously because their churches hold low expectations of financial giving—insecure church leadership and congregation cultures oriented toward avoiding possible offense soft-peddle expectations of faithful, generous giving."

- "Collective-Action Shirking: American Christians do not give money because they lack confidence that other American Christians are also contributing generously and do not want to be individually responsible for achieving collective goods."

- "Issue Privatization: Most American Christians do not give their money generously because matters of personal and family finances are highly privatized in American culture, effectively removing religious giving from any public discussion or accountability."

None of these or the other six hypotheses singularly explain why American Christians are not more generous, but each is a part of it. If we address the issue of giving being done in secret and begin to have open conversations about generosity, people will grow. They may be

2. Christian Smith, Michael O. Emerson, and Patricia Snell, *Passing the Plate: Why American Christians Don't Give Away More Money* (Oxford: Oxford University Press, 2008), 58–59.

challenged, but as long as we don't go so far as to offend anyone, we will help them to grow spiritually.

Pastors who have an issue with knowing what people give should spend time exploring their own relationship with money to figure out why that is. In the May 24, 2012, issue of *Forbes* magazine, Sheryl Nance-Nash shared in an article that the Bible mentions money more than eight hundred times. If the business world knows Jesus talked about it, we too should bring conversations about money to the forefront and not avoid them.

Joyful stewardship is one of the greatest gifts we can offer others in our faith community. We invite others into prayerful conversation about finding their hearts and placing their treasure in the midst of our significant ministry.

It should also be noted that when we engage the conversation, we can better direct it. We are able to offer stories of abundance and help people recognize the ways in which God provides us everything that we need. If our goal is to change culture and create a culture of generosity, we will find that task incredibly difficult if we are not able to talk about it. Just as the queen can lead a hive to vibrant health when she knows the resource situation of the hive, so too congregation leaders are able to lead a congregation much more effectively when they have all the information that is available.

CHAPTER 17.

FUNDRAISING IS MINISTRY

Each bee has one specific job either throughout its lifetime or for the particular stage of life it is in. A queen has one job. She lays eggs. For female bees, the jobs are set out in progression based on age. Young bees will sometimes care for the queen, but most young bees will feed the larvae before they are capped. When they are a little older, female bees serve as the custodians of the hive. Then, shortly after they develop their stingers, they serve as guard bees in case a person or a bear tries to mess with the hive. Later, the female worker becomes a forager, leaving the hive during the day to gather pollen and nectar to help the colony thrive. The male bees have one job, and that is to fertilize the queen. If they happen to accomplish their job, they die immediately. Otherwise, they return to the hive each night before going out the next day to look for an unfertilized queen.

While bees serve distinct functions in the hive, in the church, pastors get to serve in many different roles. Pastors preach, teach, and care for the sick, those who are grieving, and others in transitions. Pastors also serve the community, reach out to newcomers, and train lay leaders. Pastors often serve on or advise committees such as finance, facility, and youth ministry. The larger the church staff, the more opportunity to focus their ministry. The smaller the church, the more roles the pastor seems to fill. In all settings, we often hear pastors mention that "seminary didn't prepare me to plunge toilets and change messages on the sign out front."

The reality is that there are plenty of roles in the church for pastors and lay members to serve. Pastors can choose to occupy themselves and their time on all kinds of tasks. But by now, I hope I have made it clear that spending time on stewardship and growing giving is essential work for pastors and for congregational stewardship teams. Growing giving is ministry. Leading people to a culture of abundance is ministry at its deepest levels. As we do stewardship well, we are proclaiming, teaching, caring, challenging, praying, mentoring, and more.

Henri Nouwen says, "Fundraising is proclaiming what we believe in such a way that we offer other people an opportunity to participate with us in our vision and mission."[1] Ponder that for a minute, and recognize the deep spiritual opportunity that Nouwen states fundraising provides to people. Nouwen goes on to say,

> From the perspective of the gospel, fundraising is not a response to a crisis. Fundraising is first and foremost a form of ministry. It is a way of announcing our vision and inviting other people into our mission. . . . Fundraising is precisely the opposite of begging. When we seek to raise funds we are not saying, "Please, could you help us out because lately it's been hard." Rather, we are declaring, "We have a vision that is amazing and exciting. We are inviting you to invest yourself through the resources God has given

1. Henri Nouwen, *A Spirituality of Fundraising* (Nashville: Upper Room, 2011), viii.

you—your energy, your prayers, and your money—in this work to which God has called us."[2]

And, finally, Nouwen says,

> In fundraising as ministry, we are inviting people into a new way of relating to their resources. By giving people a spiritual vision, we want them to experience that they will in fact benefit by making their resources available to us. We truly believe that if their gift is good only for those who receive, it is not fundraising in the spiritual sense. Fundraising from the point of view from the gospel says to people: "I will take your money and invest it in this vision only if it is good for your spiritual journey, only if it is good for your spiritual health." In other words, we are calling them to an experience of conversion. "You won't become poorer, you will become richer by giving." We can confidently declare with the Apostle Paul: "You will be enriched in every way for your great generosity" (2 Cor. 9:11).[3]

GIVING AS A HIGH CALLING

I had a donor once tell me that giving to outdoor ministry helped him take the money he made in his career and make it worth something. He shared that without giving some of it away, it was just money. The problem is, so many people are paralyzed by feeling that they don't have enough. They don't see that everything they have is a gift of God. They don't understand that where their treasures are, that's where hearts are as well (Matt 6:21).

It is our responsibility and high calling to help lead people to relating to their possessions differently. We need to help them recognize that by giving a portion of their treasures away, their hearts will be closer to God's plans in the

2. Nouwen, *Spirituality of Fundraising*, 16–17.

3. Nouwen, *Spirituality of Fundraising*, 19–20.

world. And by giving generously, they declare to themselves and the world that God has provided enough, and they don't need to worry about tomorrow. Giving money away is an opportunity, and we can invite people to do this so that they will be more engaged in ministry. We are inviting them to discover a deeper meaning for their lives. We are inviting them to see that God is most important.

Fundraising is not a necessary evil or something that we do before we get to do real ministry. When done well and with significant integrity, fundraising is proclaiming the gospel and declaring that Jesus is the Lord of life. The role of the pastor and stewardship team is to paint a picture of what a God of abundance looks like and to invite people, where they are, to begin a journey to better understand this.

A pastor once told me that a young adult told her that she wouldn't be giving to the church. The pastor didn't know what to say and was fearful to challenge this person. But what could have happened was an invitation to a journey. The pastor could have told the young person that she doesn't have to give to be a member of the church, but giving would help her recognize that God is part of the most intimate parts of her life.

We should not be afraid to be specific in our invitation to give. For reluctant givers, we can suggest they give something every time they are at church (no matter the size) and put it in an envelope so that it can be tracked. Then, we can make it a point to follow up with this person in six months and talk about their giving. We could consider asking them to increase the impact of their random giving by signing up for automatic giving. Six months later, follow up with them again. Take them out for coffee and conversation, and tell them the impact that their gifts have had on people's lives and faith development. Continue the conversation by sharing vision and dreams of what the ministry can do if they will become more generous.

Is this a lot of work? Sure it is. But in the case of the pastor and young woman above, this work is about the heart of the young adult. Telling her that she doesn't have to give will likely lead to her dropping out of church in a couple of months. Walking with her intentionally shows you care for her, love her, and want her to grow spiritually. It certainly is not the only topic of conversation to have with her about her spiritual growth, but it is a key area that can lead her on her generosity journey.

Stewardship does take work, but it is incredibly meaningful. I truly did have deeper relationships with my donors at the camps than I did when I was a pastor in the parish. Why? Because in my stewardship work I talked to people about money, which meant we talked about their dreams, passions, and fears. A recurring biblical message is to have no fear of the future (Luke 12:32) and not to worry about tomorrow (Matt 6:34). However, the more I talk to people, the more I hear stories of worry and fear. Our people need to be reminded of who God is, not for the sake of a financial gift to ministry, but for the sake of allowing them to live an abundant life. Those who are paralyzed with fear fail to live.

I never ceased to be amazed at what people would share with me as they created their giving plans. Some would recount the love they had for a parent or grandparent who taught them generosity through their examples of giving. Others would honor a friendship. Still others would make a gift in memory of a loved one I didn't even know they had lost. Still others would share that they were compelled to give in order to keep themselves from becoming greedy. Even though it was hard, they did it because they didn't like who they became when they lived only for themselves. You will experience examples like this and more when you treat fundraising as ministry and dig deeper into the lives of our people.

One of the first rules I have as people make a gift visit is that the visitor should breathe deeply and pray. This isn't a gimmick or shallow exercise. I have been overwhelmed on numerous occasions before a conversation about giving. In those moments I prayed that God would go before me in the visit. Sure enough, during many visits the donor would ask me a challenging question or tell me of things I had not known. From somewhere, I was given the words to respond. I have regularly sensed God's presence in the room during a visit about money. It is a truly special opportunity, and yes, I would call it holy work.

"Where your treasure is, there your heart will be also" (Matt 6:21). We live in a world that continues to try to convince us that we live on the edge of scarcity. Yet, we have a God who emptied a tomb, fed five thousand from just a few loaves of bread and a couple of fish, turned water into wine, and enabled hundreds to be baptized in a single day. We have a God who created a marvelous world full of every abundance that we can ever imagine. This is the world that we need to share with our people. This is the God that needs to be introduced to people. This is the way we help people make a difference in the world. This is the way we convince people that there is a world of abundance and that they may live fully in that abundance.

CONCLUSION

A strong hive of honeybees will store up enough honey each spring and summer to get the colony through the winter, with enough left over to give a nice supply to the beekeeper. In addition, the flowers and gardens within a few miles of the hive will be pollinated, leading to a balance in the ecosystem where everything thrives.

Churches that live in abundance will live out their mission, give volunteers fulfilling work, have enough resources to dream new ways to reach into their communities, and have leaders who are growing in their roles, all of which contributes to being vital communities where the good news of Jesus Christ is made known.

Our world is constantly changing. Therefore, the leadership in our congregations must constantly change and adapt with the world. The Ten Steps are timeless steps to repeat as you continually lead your congregation toward living in abundance in whatever situation you face. This book seeks to reinforce three key steps:

1. Organize the council and staff for effectiveness.

2. Establish the financial stewardship program.

3. Prepare the strategic ministry vision.

You can begin leading your congregation into a state of abundance where it starts to look at challenges not as roadblocks to success but as opportunities to impact the world with the good news.

This is ongoing work. We don't just organize the council once. We don't just establish our stewardship program and then never adjust it. We don't do a strategic plan this year and then forget about it. We keep coming back to each of these steps and continue to work at them. To reach for excellence, which I believe the gospel demands of us, we keep working at it. As the world changes, so will our tactics, but the steps along the journey will stay the same.

Here is a final story to give you some hope.

A congregation in a mill town in North Carolina had taken out quite a large mortgage for a building expansion just before the economy in the area collapsed, and several of the mills closed down. For many years, they figured out how to pay the mortgage, but nothing much new happened. Everyone just hoped that they would continue to keep the doors open.

About a decade later, they called a new pastor. He rearranged the staff roles to align with the gifts of the people. They launched a new ministry to send local non-member kids to camp. He led the council in defining their roles. Then, in partnership with the judicatory, he joined a Stewardship for All Seasons group.

In the first year, this congregation grew revenue by 27.5 percent, which gave them some breathing space in their budget to pay salaries, keep health insurance coverage, and generally keep the church going forward. It gave them the hope to talk about the future. It was the first time revenue was projected to increase in over a decade.

As we talked about the future, everyone knew that the mortgage payments stood in the way of being able to dream. So the stewardship team, fresh off its victory, decided they should do what I call a "Principal Party" and pay down $25,000 of their mortgage principal. I challenged them to quadruple that goal and go for $100,000. After the six weeks of the special appeal, they exceeded $100,000, which moved their debt-free date up by at least a year. But it didn't end there.

Once the congregation reached this level of generosity, a couple in the congregation approached the pastor and said, "You know, we received an inheritance, and we have decided to tithe it to the church." They chose the church because it had a plan. This saved the church one more year of payments. But that's still not the end of the story.

Within a couple days the pastor opened his mail. In it was a check for $100,000 from a nonmember the pastor had met years before and who appreciated the pastor's work. The note said, "I meant to send this earlier, but I got busy. I'm excited about what you are doing at the church, and I wanted to help out." The pastor has told me that the finance committee is actually "giddy"—an emotion I have never personally experienced from a finance team! And the leadership of the council is eager to dive deeper into strategic planning now. They aren't stopping because getting the debt under control or out of the way has never been the goal. The goal has always been what can happen after that.

This story may seem extreme if you are currently living in a scarcity world. However, I am blessed to be part of stories like this throughout my daily work. As congregations shift from living from a survival mentality to living into the abundance that matches our understanding of God, the kingdom can truly expand, and the activity of God in front of us will be magnified.

Effective stewardship takes work. The world we live in today demands that we work at changing our cultures of scarcity into cultures of abundance. That won't happen if we don't strive for excellence. I don't expect stewardship to become the main activity in your parish, but I do expect it to be tended to with intention and purpose. This takes work and repetition. Pastors and laypeople alike must be committed to working at this, even if it turns out to be a little uncomfortable. The rewards are tremendous, but like anything, without intentional effort we will be disappointed in the outcome.

Culture changes slowly. In a year, you may experience some strong results, but it takes intention over time to shift church culture toward abundant generosity. This is a matter of the heart, and changing hearts takes prayerful and purposeful time and care. Let's change the culture around money and live as if we believe Jesus's words in Matthew 6:21 that "where your treasure is, there your heart will be also." Let's get people's hearts aligned much closer with God's ministry in this world.

APPENDIX A: OUTCOME STORIES

Here are the key items for consideration when deciding on an outcome story and developing it.

- Start with a clear story that shows how someone experienced God in his or her life in a profound manner.

- Discern the key needs of people you are writing for, and align the story with needs that people have. When I was working at camp, I knew that parents wanted their children to have a faith that would sustain them through even the toughest situations in life. We also knew that they wanted to know their children were being loved unconditionally. Therefore, we looked for stories that reinforced these key needs.

- Define the ministry goals that activities are supposed to address. Then, look for stories that indicate that you are achieving these goals through the activity.

It is also important to look ahead at the calendar of upcoming ministry activities and decide ahead of time where you will be looking for stories. Certainly, youth trips are key places. However, so are Bible studies, special worship services, and other new ministry opportunities that you are launching.

Determining how to communicate outcome stories is also critical. They can be shared live in worship as a bit of a "testimony." They can also be videotaped so the words and voice of the one impacted really convey the feeling behind the outcome. Sharing these stories in writing also works. When doing so, focus on the headline and the opening statement to draw people into the article. Often, you can pull a quote from the witness statement to draw people in. Or including a picture of the person being quoted can also help draw people to the words on the page.

EXAMPLE OUTCOME STORIES

What follows are examples of outcome stories that you can use to guide your own outcome story creation. The first story is a recent outcome story that the NC Synod of the ELCA shared. It received 418 page views, which is 200 more views than typical articles they post to their website. The goal of the article is to connect the raising up of leaders with the synod-sponsored youth event.

"I Wouldn't Be Who, or Where, I Am Today without LYO"
Lutheran Youth Organization (LYO) has always been committed to equipping leaders for the sake of sharing the Gospel.
Picture a weekend in late February filled with the organized chaos of a giant game of "rock, paper, scissors" with about five hundred old and new friends; music led by a band of teenagers that are fairly new musicians and a few adults who care deeply about them and the music they play and sing; faith stories and reflections shared by some of the brightest and best ninth through twelfth graders around; a

bishop who tosses out free T-shirts and preaches/presides at worship; intentional faith formation in small groups; 129 pizzas consumed as a late-night snack; and lots of fun and very little sleep. This is just a snapshot of what happens at the NC Synod's annual LYO Assembly. And for the past twenty-five years, Deacon Tammy Jones West, Assistant to the Bishop, has been the staff person responsible for this yearly event.

LYO of the NC Synod is open to all youth in grades 6 to 12. Youth are members by virtue of being a member of any NC Synod ELCA congregation. Every year, Lutheran youth across North Carolina gather in February for an assembly. At LYO Assembly, youth spend time with each other in small groups, singing with the band and growing in faith. The strength of LYO in North Carolina comes from the youth themselves. The LYO Board (board members are grades 9–12) see to it that LYO Assembly is always youth-planned and youth-led.

Chandler Carriker was a high school senior when he served as the LYO president from 1995 to 1996. "I'm pretty sure it was Tammy's first year, and maybe we had just transitioned from LYNC (Lutheran Youth in North Carolina) to LYO." Following high school, Chandler graduated from North Carolina State University and Lutheran Theological Southern Seminary, worked eight summers on staff at Lutheridge and Lutherock, including two summers as associate program director, and is a deacon in the ELCA. He recently left his call at Lutheran World Relief and accepted a call as the vice president of program and engagement at Novus Way Ministries. Deacon Carriker shares, "My time as an LYO president continues to be a foundation for all of the leadership opportunities I've had in the twenty-five years since then. I experienced letting people down, and how to learn from that and grow better as a team. I experienced the joy of achieving goals as a team. And I learned from leaders like Tammy, who placed the grace of Jesus at the center of what they do. Those things have always stayed with me."

Likewise, Ethan Overcash, a seminarian from Faith

Lutheran Church in Faith, North Carolina, who is currently completing his internship at Grace, Boone, served on the LYO Board from 2007 to 2009. Ethan shares, "I wouldn't be who, or where, I am today without LYO. I certainly wouldn't be in the seminary process. LYO opened the doors of the church to me and gave me a place to belong where I could discover and use the gifts God has given me. LYO empowers youth to serve and lead, and I discovered my call to ministry while serving on the LYO board. Through LYO, I discovered that the church is so much bigger than my own small-town congregation, and my understanding of the church as a whole will forever be impacted by the church I witnessed in the holy places of LYO. I continually give thanks to God for the gift of ministry that is Deacon Tammy and LYO!"

This year after the LYO Assembly, where those gathered gave thanks for Tammy's twenty-five years of service with the children, youth, and adults of this synod (and beyond), she shared in a Facebook post, "So grateful for the past twenty-five years serving in the NC Synod. The friends who became family and the job that became a call to ministry. Thank you LYO 2019 for the beautiful new stole and the ELCA frame with all the memories and journeys yet to come. Tired but blessed."

LYO has always been committed to equipping leaders for the sake of sharing the gospel. Whether the gospel is shared by someone in a youth leadership position that becomes a call to ministry, someone in a job that becomes a call to ministry, or by youth and adults who are equipped for leadership, LYO is truly equipping leaders for the church now and in years to come.

This outcome story is effective because of the personal stories shared. Outcome stories don't have to be this long. I favor the method of sharing outcome stories in worship at the time of the offering. As you start collecting the offering, share a thirty-second outcome. I remember visiting a Baptist church in Orlando where the pastor walked forward with the plates and said something along the following lines.

> Suggestion: Before we receive this week's offering, I want to share quickly how your gifts last week made a difference. A single mom had stopped for help because her car broke down. We were able to use your gifts to buy the part for her car, and some of our members installed the part. She can now get her kids to school and herself to work. Here is a portion of a thank-you note she sent: "Pastor, I want to express my thanks for helping me get my life back in order as you helped me fix my car. You and your members showed me what love and compassion look like. Thank you."

Outcome stories don't have to be from your own ministry; they can be shared from other settings. Many churches offer space to outside groups such as Head Start or Alcoholics Anonymous. Though there are confidentiality concerns with these groups, the leaders can share stories with you. I once heard a pastor share that he was stopped in the hallway of his church building by someone from AA. The man said, "Preacher, I just want to thank you for saving my life." Needless to say, this statement caught the pastor's attention. The man went on to say he is confident that without AA, he would be dead now, and he credits the church with saving his life because they offered the space for him to stay sober. Telling this story to the congregation gave them a sense of the impact of sharing their space and helped them see a "ministry" value that far exceeded any inconveniences that hosting the group may cause them.

Always be on the lookout for outcome stories in the ministry that you are doing and ways the lives of people in your congregation are being impacted. If you are having trouble finding these stories, you might want to consider whether you are truly carrying out your mission and vision. Often, discovering outcome stories is just a simple matter of asking people to tell how God, the life of faith, or some aspect of your ministry has made a difference in their lives.

APPENDIX B: SAMPLE OFFERING TALKS

I like to teach during worship. To get people to hear something in a new way, I insert a short teaching moment during the worship service. Some would call this narrative liturgy. I like to keep it short and simple. I use what I call Offering Talks as short, thirty-second teaching moments to highlight reasons that we give. Here are eight Offering Talk examples that I have written.

TALK #1: OFFERING AS AN ACT OF WORSHIP

How many of you think of the offering as an interruption to the service where we take a break in order to make certain we can pay the bills by collecting your money? Trinity Seminary professor Mark Powell shares in his book *Giving to God* that we should look at collecting the offering differently. He sees the offering as the high point of the liturgy. It is the point where we can most fully participate in the service ourselves . . . by giving up something that we value. The offering itself is an act of worship. By placing something we value in the offering plate, we are putting more of ourselves into worship. It isn't about paying the bills. It is about proclaiming that compared to God, our stuff doesn't matter.[1]

TALK #2: THE OLD TESTAMENT TITHE: WE DON'T NEED EVERYTHING WE HAVE

If we lived during the Old Testament times, and even when Jesus walked this earth, the offering would be a much more dramatic and messy part of the service. Animals would lose their lives, and sacrifices would get burned. It would get smoky in here! I'm glad we have moved on in our stewardship practices. However, have we lost something by just putting some money in the plate? By burning offerings on the altar or sacrificing an animal and not receiving money for it, we were proclaiming that God had provided us enough and that we didn't need to keep all that we had. In fact, much of what was offered to God was virtually destroyed. It wasn't sold to feed the hungry or to cover the salary of the priest. The tithe proved that we didn't need all of the abundance provided to us. Maybe we have lost something by just passing the plate.

TALK #3: IS IT OURS, OR IS IT GOD'S?

American theology tells us that however much money we are able to earn is ours. You can find this brand of the theology of wealth in the sermons of Joel Osteen, as one example, and it is reinforced by many of our politicians. Personal property is an American value. It is not aligned with Luther's understanding of our relationship with our stuff. As we proclaim the Apostles' Creed, we

1. Mark Allan Powell, *Giving to God: The Bible's Good News about Living a Generous Life* (Grand Rapids: Eerdmans, 2006), 9–22.

state that God is the Creator. Most of us believe this. Luther's explanation of this is that all of our gifts and abilities come from God. Therefore, everything that we have comes from the gifts God gives us. Sometimes, we like to think stuff is ours and that we do things ourselves. However, isn't it nice that we don't have to be God? Isn't it nice that we just have to be good stewards of the gifts that God provides us? I know that I have enough to worry about that I am thrilled that I don't have to worry about being God too. I prefer to think of my role in life to be a steward of what God provides me. And if that is how it is, shouldn't we look at our "stuff" differently? We should look at it as taking care of God's stuff.

TALK #4: REGULAR AND SMART GIVING

Establishing a plan for regular giving is important. People who take the time to complete a statement of intent (pledge) or establish a regular pattern for giving, such as using Simply Giving or setting up a recurring gift from their bank account, give on average ten times more than those whose giving isn't intentional or regular. The difference has nothing to do with wealth. It has everything to do with intentionality. One dollar per day is $365 over the course of the year, and you can see by the charts we have included in the bulletin that we have many people who give less than $1 per day. Regular, systematic giving is the easiest way to move up to a new giving category.

There are also some smart ways to give. If you are 70.5 years old or older, you can give directly from your IRA to the church and satisfy your Required Minimum Distribution, but you do not have to declare it as income. If you have a stock or mutual fund that has increased in value, you can donate it, claim the tax deduction for the gift, and avoid the capital gains. I think God wants us to be generous. I think God also wants us to be smart about the ways we share the resources that have been entrusted to us.

TALK #5: SEEK IN PRAYER GOD'S WILL FOR YOUR GIVING

We often hear people say, "My giving is between me and God." Well, they are right. However, we have to be careful to make certain that this is not a place where God's voice sounds too much like our own. There is that one pesky Scripture reading in Luke 18:22, where Jesus tells the rich man to sell everything and give it to the poor. Because we have heard God's voice say that, sometimes we may put up our defenses and not let the voice of God have much room in the conversation about our giving.

Well, we need to make sure that prayer is a dialogue. We don't need to create God in our own image. We need to listen to what God calls us to do. Spiritual growth happens when we are challenged, look beyond ourselves, and open ourselves up to responding to God in new ways. It is true in our giving as well. This year, pray about your giving. I don't think God will tell you to sell everything. But as you prayerfully consider your giving, you will discover new ways to grow in generosity. God may show you how you can give something up in your life. Or perhaps God will show you how to have more faith in tomorrow and not hold on to so much because of worry.

The church will once again send you a letter inviting you to grow in your giving. I invite you to listen to that letter and see if you can hear the voice of God in the ask.

TALK #6: FEAR NOT

The words of Jesus in Matthew 6 can help ease our biggest fears.

> Therefore, I say to you, don't worry about your life, what you'll eat or what you'll drink, or about your body, what you'll wear. Isn't life more than food and the body more than clothes? Look at the birds in the sky. They don't sow seed or harvest grain or gather crops into barns. Yet your heavenly Father feeds them. Aren't you worth much more than they are? Who among you by worrying can add a single moment to your life? And why do you worry about clothes? Notice how the lilies in the field grow. They don't wear themselves out with work, and they don't spin cloth. (6:25–28)

> Do not worry about tomorrow for tomorrow will bring its own worries. Today's troubles are enough for today. (6:34)

The reality is, many of us do fear. We worry about not having enough. We fear that we could lose it all. We often ask "What if?" as we make decisions to spend money or give money away in the church. But the truth is, we have been blessed. God is creator. Luther says that means that God provides us with whatever we need. Therefore, since God created us, we are free to worry a bit less. We can trust that we are more valuable than the birds of the air, and we can live as Jesus says, not worrying about tomorrow.

How would your giving to the church be different if you worried a little less about tomorrow and simply lived today as if God provides abundantly?

TALK #7: DECIDE TO GIVE SACRIFICIALLY

Little is ever accomplished without sacrifice. This is true in our homes, work, churches, and country. Sacrifice is a necessary component of abundant living. And so it is with the Christian life and faith. Our salvation cost God the cross. Bonhoeffer rightly said there is no cheap grace.

Often, church giving is only token giving, averaging about 2 percent of income. No wonder there is so little joy or satisfaction in it. It requires no sacrifice! We have given only what we could easily afford, what we would not really miss.

Experience has shown many that giving, to be meaningful and joyful, also has to be sacrificial. Each of us will have to determine what amount or percentage is sacrificial for our own circumstances.

Jesus says in Matthew 6:21, "Where your treasure is, there your heart will be also." As we approach our stewardship drive this year, perhaps we can focus a bit more on where we want our heart. As we seek to connect our hearts more closely with God's work through this congregation, perhaps we can increase our giving to live out Jesus's words of this text.

TALK #8: OPPORTUNITIES

It is pretty clear in the Bible that Jesus says to feed the hungry, comfort the grieving, and care for the widow and orphan. Some of us have a passion for passing on faith to children. Others have a passion for raising up leaders for the church. Still others want to see non-Christians experience the good news for the first time.

As we think about where we want to get involved, we cannot do it all. However, as we financially support our congregation this year, we are involved in all of this. Not all of us are called to be teachers, but offerings support teaching and passing on faith to kids. Not all of us have the gifts to comfort the grieving, but our financial gifts provide for great pastoral care. Not all of us have the time to go out and feed the hungry, but we can all give significantly according to our means so that the hungry can be fed.

Our congregation directly engages in many of these ministries on our own. Others, we are able to accomplish through the synod as they carry on work for the God's kingdom on our behalf. As we continue to grow the ministry, we have more and more opportunities to engage in different ministries right here and across the region, the nation, and the globe.

When we financially support the ministry here, our gifts make possible the many ways we engage in ministry. Even if you are not personally serving in a particular ministry, your gifts make that ministry possible. As we give generously, we have the opportunity and the privilege to feed the hungry, care for the grieving, pass on faith to children, raise up leaders, and so much more.

APPENDIX C: SAMPLE STRATEGIC PLANS, GOALS, OBJECTIVES, AND TACTICS

As described in chapters 3–5, creating a strategic vision is essential to the health and flourishing of your congregation. That vision needs to be supported by clear goals. In turn, each goal requires key objectives and tactics to accomplish the objectives. Below you will find examples of a goal supported by objectives and tactics. These plans were created for particular congregations, so it is not intended for you to take these goals and apply them to your congregation. All good strategic planning is contextual.

SAMPLE NUMBER 1

Goal: To grow first-time worship attendees by 104 per year by December 31, 2023.
   Objectives to reach the goal:

1. Implement effective tracking of first-time visitors and all nonmembers by January 2021.

2. Create a comprehensive marketing program by July 2021.

3. Create a culture of invitation by October 2022.

Tactics to reach each objective:

1. Implement effective tracking of first-time visitors and all nonmembers by January 2021.
   a. Utilize church management software to keep up with the data.
   b. Provide weekly progress to outreach team.
   c. Provide monthly progress to council and congregation.
   d. Hire a staff person to work with marketing program, culture of invitation, and tracking.

2. Create a comprehensive marketing program by July 2021.
   a. Attain a Google grant.
   b. Determine Google keywords and apply to website, and purchase Google advertisements with grant.
   c. Determine Facebook characteristics to reach as well as times to post.
   d. Purchase Facebook ads, and boost stories around events.
   e. Attain a "needs assessment" from the most recent twenty visitors to determine what needs they were looking to have fulfilled by attending worship.
   f. Purchase lists of people new to your community, fitting target demographics.
   g. Attain yard signs for members to place in their yards inviting to Easter, Christmas

Eve, and start of school year worship services.

h. Place banners of invitation in the church building inviting nonmembers using the facility to worship on key dates.

i. Implement roadside signage around key invitation dates.

j. Share invitation for each member.

k. Sponsor two days on local NPR station the week prior to Christmas Eve and the week prior to Easter.

l. Hire a staff person to work with marketing program, culture of invitation, and tracking.

3. Create a culture of invitation by October 2022.

a. Monthly ask for names of people to invite, and begin praying for them at least six weeks ahead of invitation. Attain at least twenty-four names per month (three names for each needed successful invitation).

b. Mail invitations to each key service and as general invitation to join. Mail each person at least four times before removing them from list.

c. Offer training to members in different settings to teach how to identify and invite people to worship.

d. Share a monthly outcome story of a successful invitation and share by video just to members so they can learn from it.

e. Have those who have been invited and come to worship share how it felt to be invited and welcomed. Share these quotes in print material and verbally.

f. Hire a staff person to work with marketing program, culture of invitation, and tracking.

SAMPLE NUMBER 2

Goal: By December 31, 2024, build a children and youth program that results in graduating high school seniors having an articulate faith that is capable of sustaining them through life's challenges.

Objectives to reach the goal:

1. Develop a confirmation program that engages 100 percent of youth for at least two hundred contact hours prior to final confirmation ritual.

2. Provide a comprehensive youth program that engages all high school youth in at least two weekend retreats per year and eight key activities per year.

3. Engage 75 percent of children and middle school youth in regular participation in at least one key ongoing program of the church.

Tactics to reach each objective:

1. Develop a confirmation program that engages 100 percent of youth for at least two hundred contact hours prior to confirmation.

   a. Study confirmation programs of similar size and demographic, and report back.

b. Visit in the home of each family six months prior to starting confirmation to share the purpose of the program with parents and the outcomes you are seeking.

c. Develop and sign covenants about confirmation.

d. Partner with local outdoor ministry to provide weekend retreats as a significant part of confirmation program or as makeup sessions for those who miss other scheduled programs.

e. Provide each student with a mentor who is trained to share his or her faith and help confirmands articulate their faith in daily life.

f. Provide a capstone week of summer camp for confirmation.

g. Follow up in the homes of the confirmed and their families three months following confirmation to discuss how they plan to live out their faith in high school.

2. Provide a comprehensive youth program that engages all high school youth in at least two weekend retreats per year and eight key activities per year.

a. Develop five key weekend retreats per year that blend service, relationships, and faith development. Register each youth for a minimum of two retreats.

b. Develop twenty key youth activities per year, and have youth commit to attending at least eight activities during the year. Activities should offer a blend of service, relationship, and faith-development activities.

c. Monitor progress toward appropriate level of participation on a quarterly basis. Youth committee contacts families falling short of covenanted number of activities.

d. Evaluate each activity for the desired purpose upon completion.

3. Engage 75 percent of children and middle school youth in regular participation in at least one key ongoing program of the church.

a. Develop youth/children choir, youth/children chime choir, youth/children service team, and youth/young youth groups.

b. Youth committee develops a tracking mechanism to track each youth's participation.

c. Contact quarterly anyone in these age groups not signed up at least twice per year to invite them to an area of interest.

d. Encourage youth/children to invite unconnected children/youth at least once per year to an area of interest.

e. Contact parents of unconnected children/youth contacted twice per year—once in person and once by phone to remind of the faith development goals that are being advanced in each area.

f. Evaluate each program for its effectiveness based on sharing faith, building community, and helping to build a lasting faith.

Related tactics:

a. Contact college students each year of their college career, and have them describe what activities in church helped provide the faith they need to thrive in college. Seek stories of how students are living out their faith in college and how their time with their home congregation equipped them for the journey into adulthood. Share these stories with youth, parents, and the congregation. Be sure to keep track of students who have graduated from the youth program but did not attend college. How did their experience in the church youth group impact their daily lives?

b. Monitor the growth of the program on a semi-annual basis, and add a children's/youth staff person when fifty children/youth are actively engaged in the program.